THE STUDY OF ARABIC IN MALTA
1632 to 1915

THE STUDY OF ARABIC IN MALTA
1632 to 1915

Dionisius AGIUS

Translated from Maltese
by Vinċenz P. Borg

Revised and edited
by Francine Geraci

PEETERS

LOUVAIN

1990

D. 1990/0602/76

ISBN 90-6831-260-X

THE STUDY OF ARABIC IN MALTA: 1632 to 1915

Dionisius Agius
Translated by Vinċenz P. Borg
Revised and Edited by Francine Geraci

First published in Maltese. *Malta, Ċentru għat-Tagħlim ta' l-Għarbi fil-Mediter-rann*
by Klabb Kotba Maltin, 1980 (Number 102)
Dewey 492.77'707'04585

CONTENTS

Preface VII

Abbreviations IX

Introduction XI

Chapter I
Foundations of the Study of Arabic in Malta 1

Chapter II
The Teaching of Arabic at the University of Malta . . . 11

Chapter III
Arabic Works in Language and Culture 22
(a) The first collections of Oriental manuscripts 22
(b) Early Arabic linguistic works 24
(c) Arabic literary works by Maltese authors 28

Manuscripts (Arabic, Turkish, and Persian) and Publications . 31

Lecturers of Arabic in Malta, 1632-1915 39

Appendix 40

Bibliography 43

Index 49

PREFACE

This study is based on two research works: one by Ettore Rossi, "Manoscritti e documenti orientali nelle biblioteche e negli archivi di Malta" [*Archivio Storico di Malta*, 2, i (1930): 1-10], the other by Antonio Cremona, "L'Antica Fondazione della Scuola di Lingua Araba in Malta" [an extract from *Melita Historica*, I, ii-iv (1953): 3-21]. There have been several other publications on this subject during the last forty years, but as they have only repeated what had been recorded before by Rossi and Cremona in the works referred to above, the have added nothing new.

With this in mind, I determined to examine all sources thoroughly to produce as comprehensive a study as possible. I have gone through all records kept by the Inquisition, the Church in Malta, and the Propaganda Fide in Rome for information related to the teaching of Arabic before the occupation of the island by the French under Napoleon. For the period following, namely the British administration up to 1914/15, I have consulted the records in the National Library and the library of the University of Malta.

For the preparation of this text, I am greatly indebted to Patri Ġorġ Aquilina, O.F.M. (Librarian, Franciscan Provincial Library, Valletta), Dun Ġwann Azzopardi (Archivist, the Archives of the Cathedral Museum, Mdina), Pawlu Xuereb (Librarian, the University of Malta), F.X. Mallia (former Director of the National Museum, Valletta), V.A. Depasquale (former Librarian, the National Library, Valletta), and Pawlu Mizzi (Director, Klabb Kotba Maltin).

Last but not least, I should like to thank G.M. Wickens and E. Birnbaum, Professors of Islamic Studies in the Department of Middle East and Islamic Studies at the University of Toronto, for their encouragement and expert advice.

DIONISIUS AGIUS
University of Leeds
1989

ABBREVIATIONS

AIM	*Archives of the Inquisition, Malta*
CAM	*Cathedral Archives, Malta*
APF	*Archives of the Propaganda Fide, Rome*
FPAM	*Franciscan Provincial Archives, Malta*
AOSJ	*Archives of the Order of St. John, Malta*
AUM	*Archives of the University of Malta*
NLM	*National Library, Malta*
BML	*British Museum, London*

INTRODUCTION

The Christian world began to show interest in the study of the Arabic language after the Reformation, during the economic revival of the seventeenth century. The Ottoman Empire had become a major force, widespread and powerful as it was, dominating much of Eastern Europe and all Arab countries. The Eastern Mediterranean had been transformed into an Ottoman sea, dividing Europe. Once more the Cross was pitted against the Crescent. But in addition to the religious rivalry between East and West, political jealousy also fuelled this division. Sixteenth century western Europe felt threatened as the Ottoman Empire continually strengthened itself economically, religiously, and even militarily through the *yeni çeri* (Janissaries), Muslim converts from Christianity who became the elite military corps in the Islamic world. It was over such an empire that Süleymân II Kânûnî (1520-1566), known in the West as "the Magnificent", ruled during the Ottoman Golden Age.

But by the beginning of the seventeenth century, the Ottoman Empire no longer controlled the world's political scene, owing largely to a disorganised central government and lack of discipline in its armies. The Christian world, on the other hand, was regaining its lost dominance. This can be attributed to several factors: (a) the discovery of America, (b) the agricultural revolution, (c) technological advances during the Age of Enlightenment, and (d) the highly organised and centralised governments throughout Europe.

The Ottoman Empire, realising its weaknesses, began to relinquish its political and economic hold first on the Arab states, then on Eastern Europe, until it finally shrank to what is known today as Turkey. The Arabs, enjoying their newly acquired freedom from the Turks, soon resumed trade with Christian Europe, a commerce which had long been prohibited. Christian merchants travelling to Arab countries were accompanied by self-proclaimed "missionaries". But while the merchants found the *lingua franca* quite suitable for their commercial needs on the shores of Arab countries, this language proved useless to the missionaries in the hinterland.

Chiefly for this reason, the ecclesiastical authorities in Rome argued that if a college where missionaries could study Arabic were established, many difficulties would be solved, and the propagation of the Christian faith made easier. The Franciscan Fathers took the initiative to organise such a study of Arabic. On April 25, 1622, Tomaso Obicini (fl. 1630), a Franciscan from Novara, authorised by a decree from the Sacra Congregazione de Propaganda Fide, opened the college in Montario, Rome. Even Pope Urban VIII (1623-1644) showed interest in this project, and set up a college in Rome for the propagation of faith through missionaries. These, having first been trained at the colleges in Rome, were sent to various Muslim countries. But the Franciscans were already planning to establish other such centres outside Rome, and it was then that they expressed the desire to begin the study of Arabic in Malta.

Chapter I

FOUNDATIONS OF THE STUDY OF ARABIC IN MALTA

The study of Arabic in Malta was begun by the Franciscans in Valletta in 1632[1]. The lecturer was Patri Franġisk Flieles, who had been commissioned by the Sacra Congregazione in Rome through a reference sent on February 13, 1628[2]. There was no designated location where the Franciscan could teach Arabic, although the Franciscan Fathers were satisfied using their monastery for this purpose[3].

According to Pawlu Mallia, Arabic was also being taught at the Jesuit College in Valletta[4]. There are no records identifying the lecturer, and it is possible Patri Franġisk taught there as well. Most probably the Jesuits had their own lecturer of Arabic, as in those days, according to Pawlu Mallia, Jesuits travelled on galleys, teaching Muslim slaves the rudiments of the Christian faith[5]. In fact, the dispatching of Jesuits to Malta to bring Christianity to the Muslims had been the wish of the founder of the Society of Jesus, Inigo di Loyola (1491-1556)[6]. But Pawlu Mallia argues that, since documents do not record that there were any Jesuits in Malta at the time who spoke either Turkish or Arabic to fulfil their mission[7], the probability was that the Jesuits used interpreters in their contacts with the Muslim slaves.

[1] APF (Roma) Lettere, vol. 12, p. 31r. E. Fenech quotes 1631 as the date when the study was begun. There were no schools prior to 1632. See "Malta's Contribution towards Arabic Studies", *Actes du Premier Congres d'Études des Cultures Méditerranéennes d'Influence Arabo-Berbère* (Alger: SNED, 1973), p. 256.

[2] "Essendo stato deputato per lator della lingua araba in questa isola fra Francesco da Malta minore osservante, questa Sacra Congregazione, che graditamente dichiara l'eretione e continuazione dello Studio della suddetta lingua, ha voluto che io a V.S. raccommandi come con ogni efficacia faccio, la persona del suddetto Padre acciò l'agiusti e col Gran Maestro e con Mons. Vescovo per l'efformazione del desiderio della medesima Sac. Congregazione incaricando V.S. della sorveliantia doveroso del medesimo studio, sine che questa lodevole opera si principii e prosequisca a gloria di Dio, et in salute di molte animi che per difecto di operarii che sappino la suddetta lingua stanno in pericolo della loro salvazione..." AIM Lettere della Sacra Congregazione de Propaganda Fide, vol. I, pp. 16, 28 (1726 Correspondence).

[3] G. Scerri, *Malta e i luoghi santi della Palestina* (Malta: 1933), p. 56.

[4] P. Mallia, *Il-Ġiżwiti* (Malta: Injazjana, 1970), p. 49. The Jesuits opened their college on November 12, 1592.

[5] P. Mallia, *op. cit.*, p. 44.

[6] P. Mallia, *op. cit.*, p. 15.

[7] P. Mallia, *op. cit.*, p. 50.

It is difficult for one to conclude whether the teaching of Arabic at the Jesuit College antedates that at the Franciscan monastery. Still, according to Ġużeppi Mizzi, it was as early as 1622, the year of its foundation in Rome[8], that the Congregazione de Propaganda Fide considered establishing the study of Arabic in Malta. But as yet no one has discoverd any records pinpointing the location on the island intended by the Congregazione for such a purpose.

According to the necrology found in the Franciscan Provincial Library in Malta, Patri Franġisk died on February 16, 1633[9]. Hence, this lecturer taught Arabic for only one year, notwithstanding the fact that interest in such a study in Malta had started much earlier[10]. "Flieles" (i.e., Mal. "chickens") may seem a dubious surname to the reader; it is highly probable that the surname "Pullicino" is an Italianised version of this Semitic name (from Arabic, Abū Falālis, "possessor of chickens")[11]. Flieles was a *targaman* (interpreter) for the Order of Saint John[12]. He also wrote a book on agriculture which he dedicated to Grandmaster Wignacourt (1601-1622) and another dedicated to Bishop Cagliares (1615-1635)[13]. A letter sent by the Sacra Congregazione shows the high esteem in which Patri Franġisk was held for his remarkable work and complete dedication[14].

Notwithstanding all this, the establishment of Arabic studies in Malta did not come easily. Many promises had been made to Flieles in

[8] G. Mizzi, "Spigolando fra documenti inediti (Sec. XVII-XIX)", *Melita Historica*, 5, i (1968): 52. In 1622, the college of S. Pietro in Montorio was opened in Rome for the teaching of Arabic.

[9] E. Fenech recorded the date of the death of Patri Franġisk incorrectly by two years. According to Fenech, Flieles died in 1635. See "Malta's Contribution ...", *art. cit.*, p. 257.

[10] AIM Diottalevi, vol. 26 (2), 1605. Proceeding 66, p. 9v. "Salīm b. Manṣūr taught Arabic to Dun Victorio Cassar".

[11] "It might be considered that the men with non-Semitic surnames grossly outnumber the ones with a Semitic surname. This however, does not necessarily imply a foreign origin of the families to which they belonged. Surnames were not acquired by natural inheritance alone, and it was quite possible for Maltese families to acquire a non-Semitic surname ... Both the clergy and the notaries, as well as the whole rest of the oligarchy ruling the island in the fifteenth and the earlier centuries, were deeply impregnated with the culture of Sicily, Spain, and Europe generally. They kept their records in a European language and tended to translate surnames as they wrote... Pullicino and Pulcello could be translations into Italian from Maltese of surnames Chetcuti or Fellase..." See G. Wettinger, "The Distribution of Surnames in Malta in 1419 and the 1480's", *Journal of Maltese Studies*, 5 (1968): 27.

[12] NLM MS 1142, p. 723.

[13] *Ibid.* One of these books was later presented to King Philip IV of Spain (1621-1665).

[14] AIM Lettere della Sacra Congregazione de Propaganda.

1628-1629[15], but apparently both the Inquisitor Nicol Herrera (1627-1630) and Bishop Cagliares were creating obstacles. This is confirmed by a letter sent by the Sacra Congregazione in Rome, urging the ecclesiastical authorities to solve all problems concerning the setting up of Arabic studies and to start the course as soon as possible[16].

In 1632, the study of Arabic was begun at the monastery of the Discalced Carmelites in Bormla[17]. Again, the lecturer here is unknown. Probably Flieles held this position, as he was often called to the Inquisitor's palace in Birgu to act as an interpreter. I have reason to believe that transport facilities between Bormla and Valletta or vice versa were made available to him, employed as he was in the double capacity of lecturer and interpreter[18]. Nor do we know who succeeded Patri Franġisk after his death in 1633. In 1637 Patri Duminku Pace was appointed lecturer. By this time, in a meeting held on April 30, 1632, the Discalced Carmelites had already decided to open a residential seminary where prospective missionaries to Muslim countries (Egypt, Syria, and Persia) would study oriental languages[19]. However it was not Patri Pace, the Franciscan, who had been appointed lecturer at the Carmelite monastery but his nephew, Dun Franġisk Azzopardi, a diocesan priest. So at that time in Malta we come across two lecturers of Arabic, conducting two concurrent courses. But since the one at the Franciscan monastery in Valletta was considered a private concern, the Inquisitor Fabio Chigi (1634-1639)[20] did his best to make the study of Arabic available to the general public. He sent letters to the Sacra Congregazione in Rome to win its support for his plans. The Sacra Congregazione complied on September 22, 1637[21].

[15] APF Lettere, vol. 8, pp. 49r-v.

[16] "Stadium linguae Arabicae in Melita insula impeditur ... Referente eodem I11. mo D. Card. S. Sixti difficultates quas haec erectio studii linguae Arabicae in Melita Insula apud Minores de Observantia S. Cong. iussit scribi Inquisitori et Episcopo eiusdem Insula, ut curent difficultates praesentes removeri, ac erigi presentem studiorum, et simul praecepit agi cum Commissario Generali pro eisdem difficultatibus tollendis". APF Acta 1629, p. 240.

[17] A. Cremona, "L'Antica Fondazione della Scuola di Lingua Araba in Malta", *Melita Historica*, I, ii-iv (1953): 4. Cremona writes that the Franciscans held their courses in Arabic at their Rabat (Malta) convent, but there are no records proving such a claim.

[18] NLM MS 1142, p. 723. Dun Franġisk Flieles was appointed interpreter for Arabic by the Order of St. John because of his skills in this language.

[19] A. Mizzi, *L'Apostolato maltese nei secoli passati con speciale riguardo all'azione missionaria svolta nel bacino mediterraneo*, vol. I (Malta: 1937), p. 40; T Somigli, *Etiopia Francescana*, I, iii (1928): 63.

[20] Later made cardinal and elected Pope, under the name of Alexander VII (1655-1667).

[21] A. Cremona, *art. cit.*, p. 22.

Patri Duminku Pace, the Franciscan, was recommended for the post of co-lecturer of Arabic in 1637 by Patri Antonio da Virgoletta. In a letter written on September 19 to Monsignor Ingoli, secretary of the Propaganda Fide, Patri Antonio said that Chigi had nominated Dun Franġisk Azzopardi as lecturer of Arabic and Patri Duminku Pace as assistant lecturer to his nephew[22].

Such a preference was motivated by several reasons. Firstly, Dun Franġisk was more competent than his uncle. Evidently he had studied Arabic at the College of the Propaganda Fide under renowned tutors, with the result that he acquired a didactic technique which was unique for those days[23]. Secondly, Malta's newly built capital city, Valletta, still lacked all kinds of facilities; Birgu, situated so close to the harbour, was still the administrative, commercial, and religious centre of the island. Thirdly, since Patri Pace, as Commissioner for the Holy Places, was already involved in a wide range of duties and responsibilities, the Inquisitor concluded that Patri Pace might help his nephew only if such need were to arise. Fourthly, students living in Valletta could attend lectures given by Patri Pace[24] without having to commute between Valletta and Birgu. All in all, as far as I can see, the Congregazione was not especially satisfied with Patri Pace's appointment, and hence most probably left the decision to the Grandmaster, the Bishop, and the Inquisitor[25]. The nomination presented great difficulties, and the Maltese ecclesiastical authorities seemed to have found a solution to avoid any possible rivalry between Patri Duminku Pace and Dun Franġisk Azzopardi, competent though they may have been in their fields.

When the Inquisitor Fabio Chigi asked the Congregazione for financial assistance so that the school might be set up and the lecturer paid, the Congregazione did not commit itself in any way but referred the Inquisitor to Jean Paul de Lascaris Castellar (1636-1657), Grandmaster of the Order, and to Giovanni Balagner Camarasa (1635-1663), Bishop of Malta and Prior of the Order, to discuss all financial matters with them[26]. After lengthy discussions with the ecclesiastical authorities, Bishop Camarasa, through his own generosity, founded a benefice referred to as "ta' l-Iskof" (i.e., an estate belonging to the Bishop) or

[22] G. Scerri, *op. cit.*, p. 58.
[23] APF Lettere, vol. 19, pp. 203-204.
[24] T. Somigli, *Etiopia Francescana*, I, i (1928): 63.
[25] APF Lettere, vol. 19, p. 217.
[26] A. Cremona, *art. cit.*, p. 22.

"ta' Santa Cecilia". The income received in the form of rents for the lands and dwellings on this estate in Għawdex was to provide for the salary of the lecturer only[27]. On his part, the assigned lecturer was bound by one of the clauses in the benefice to present an annual prize of twenty Roman *scudi* to the year's best students[28].

One cannot tell, however, whether the benefice provided also for Patri Duminku Pace in his capacity of co-lecturer in Valletta. If the teaching of Arabic in Valletta was considered a private concern, it could be that even though Patri Pace had been appointed co-lecturer to Dun Azzopardi, he was not entitled to any share of the benefice, "ta' l-Iskof".

Dun Franġisk died on September 18, 1643, after a four-year career dedicated to teaching Arabic. He was succeeded by Dun Salvu Fenech, a doctor of law, who was expected to instruct students in a place convenient for them[29]. Whether this was in Valletta, Birgu, or Mdina no one can say. But it seems that during the lectureship of Dun Salvu, up to 1663, the Franciscan, Patri Duminku Pace, was still teaching at the Valletta monastery[30].

Dun Salvu Fenech taught Arabic under the patronage of the Congregazione for forty-six years. In 1683, he resigned his lectureship to dedicate himself wholeheartedly to the welfare of his parishioners in Isla. Six years later, on May 5, 1689, he died and was buried at Mosta according to his wishes[31].

Here I must refer to a certain Patri Anġlu Xerri, a Franciscan from Rabat (Malta), who taught Arabic during this period. No exact records of his teaching career have been kept, and although the necrology of the Franciscan Provincial Library lists Xerri as a lecturer of Arabic, it is not specified whether or not he lectured in Malta[32]. He died on February 27, 1680, a few years before Dun Salvu Fenech.

The death of these two lecturers was followed by a series of events which call for a few comments. Firstly, while assuming that Patri Xerri

[27] V. Azzopardi, *Raccolta di varie cose antiche e moderne, utile ed interessanti riguardanti Malta e Gozo* (Malta: 1843), p. 140; A. Mifsud, "Appunti sugli archivi di Malta", *Archivum Melitense*, 2 (1912-13): 48. This estate is located in the limits of Għajn Sielem, Għawdex.

[28] "Iis discipulis tantum tribuentur, qui toto anni curriculo in eadem Universitate Linguae Arabicae Scholam frequentarint". *Senate Proceedings*, vol. 4, i (Malta), p. 64.

[29] A. Cremona, *art. cit.*, document H, p. 24.

[30] T. Somigli, *op. cit.*, p. 63.

[31] A. Ferres, *Descrizione storica delle chiese di Malta e Gozo* (Malta: 1866), p. 254.

[32] G. Scerri, *op. cit.*, p. 61. Edward Fenech says that Patri Xerri taught Arabic for twenty-eight years, but did not state any reference.

taught in Malta, we have not the slightest idea whether or not he was co-lecturer to Don Salvu Fenech, as Patri Dominku Pace had been to Dun Franġisk Azzopardi. Secondly (assuming that it had not been discontinued), was the course given in Valletta, causing it to lose its appeal? The question arises because the post of lecturer of Arabic in the Franciscan Order remained vacant after the death of Patri Anġlu Xerri. Thirdly, were the ecclesiastical authorities still as enthusiastic about the teaching of Arabic as they had been forty-six years earlier? It is difficult to provide definite answers. However, there can be no doubt that after the death of Dun Salvu Fenech, the Congregazione de Propaganda Fide in Rome and the ecclesiastical authorities in Malta no longer saw eye to eye.

It so happened that Bishop Mikiel Ġlormu Molina (1678-1684) wanted to amalgamate the benefice referred to as "ta' l-Iskof" with the funds pertaining to the seminary, to help with the construction of a seminary at Mdina[33]. To this effect, the Bishop sent a letter to Pope Innocent XI (1676-1689), who in turn forwarded it to the Sacra Congregazione[34]. The request was rejected by the Congregazione in Rome. The Bishop of Malta, utterly displeased with such a decision, concluded that the Congregazione as an institution was ignorant of the financial needs of a country which, for the first time in its history, was striving to build a seminary for Maltese priests to strengthen the local diocese. The Bishop was correct, but it must be borne in mind that the primary goal of the Congregazione was to establish the study of Arabic to facilitate the propagation of the Christian faith among Arab Muslims, not to meet the needs of a particular diocese. On the other hand, the Congregazione failed to realize that the benefice had been founded by the Bishop's predecessor, Bishop Camarasa himself, and that the income from the estate was the fruit of the sweat and toil of the people of Malta and Għawdex. The Congregazione decided that instead of wasting time with idle words, it would be better to take some action and select a lecturer of Arabic. An official notice calling for applications to fill the vacancy was published, and interviews were held on March 10, 1684. Dun Fabrizju Bonnici was given the appointment, and hence made eligible for the benefice in question[35]. In 1688, the Archdeacon Dun Mikiel Bonnici convened the Cathedral Chapter to review

[33] A. Cremona, *art. cit.*, p. 10.
[34] *Ibid.*
[35] *Ibid.*

the situation regarding the construction of the seminary and to discuss, among other matters, the "ta' l-Iskof" benefice.

On October 17, 1688, two letters signed by all members of the Chapter, which then consisted of twenty-three canons and twenty diocesan priests from Isla, were sent to Bishop David Cocco Palmieri (1684-1713), who at that time was in Rome. The letters emphasised the urgent need to have a seminary built for the good of the whole diocese[36]. This request was again rejected[37].

After the death of Bishop Ġakmu Cannaves (1713-1722), this proposition was revived by Bishop Gaspare Gori Mancini (1722-1728) and Inquisitor Antonio Ruffo (1720-1728), who was later elected to the Sacred College of Cardinals. Both were of the opinion that once the "ta' l-Iskof" benefice became integrated with the seminary funds, the teaching of Arabic could take place in the same institution[38], with the added advantage that the benefits from such studies would not be limited only to seminarians but could be made available also to lay people. Both the Bishop and the Inquisitor agreed that the Congregazione should continue to appoint the lecturer, following interviews held for that purpose[39].

The reply from Rome was again negative. In a letter dated April 16, 1725, Cardinal Sacripante, secretary of the Congregazione, informed Bishop Mancini that the Council members of the Congregazione were of the opinion that for the time being, it was not appropriate for the benefice to be amalgamated with the seminary funds[40]. But in the meantime, while Bishop Mancini awaited a reply from Rome, he had the benefice transferred to the seminary without permission. Whilst the majority of the Maltese ecclesiastics had agreed with the Bishop's proposal, others opposed it. According to Ninu Cremona, Dun Fabrizju Bonnici, the lecturer of Arabic, sent a letter to Rome protesting that as the benefice had been founded exclusively for the benefit of the lecturer, the Bishop's proposal should on no account be accepted[41]. Dun Bonnici was only looking after his own interests in taking such an initiative; he feared that this salary from the benefice would be drastically reduced if the benefice were ever to be administered by the

[36] CAM MS 174, p. 265.
[37] NLM MS 2, p. 625.
[38] CAM MS 174, p. 374.
[39] CAM MS 174, p. 375.
[40] AIM (Secretariat) Correspondence, vol. 8, p. 323.
[41] A. Cremona, *art. cit.*, p. 25.

seminary. Needless to say, the Congregazione agreed with the lecturer, and sent the Maltese ecclesiastical authorities its usual negative reply.

According to Vinċenzo Borg, this refusal from Rome was the last: after this episode, no other attempt was made to hand over the benefice to the seminary[42].

Arabic was being taught in Valletta for one hour a day, except on Sundays and feast days[43]. The exact location, while unknown, could have been the Franciscan monastery, as in earlier days when the Franciscans had their own lecturer. According to the correspondence referred to above between Dun Fabrizju Bonnici and the Congregazione, which now forms part of the Cathedral Archives at Mdina, Dun Bonnici acted also as an interpreter for the Inquisition at Birgu[44]. The Congregazione preferred to have someone who was both well-versed in Arabic and a Christian occupying this position at the Inquisitor's court, as Muslim Arabs had occasionally been called in to act in this capacity[45]. This had been the cause of much concern: when the Inquisition submitted a report of its investigations to Rome, the Congregazione, in a letter to Malta dated September 30, 1724, did not hesitate to make its worries known[46].

Dun Fabrizju Bonnici died in 1729, after teaching Arabic for forty-years. He was the third lecturer at the school established by the Propaganda Fide.

That same year Dun Girgor Carbone was chosen as the successor of Dun Bonnici. He started teaching in Valletta, as had been the practice with previous lecturers, but he had to submit to one condition which the new Bishop, Pawlu Alferan de Bussan (1728-1758), imposed upon him. Dun Carbone was asked to teach both at Valletta and Mdina at the newly completed seminary, alternating on a weekly basis[47]. The Bishop wanted to introduce Arabic in the seminary curriculum and concluded that it would be far easier for the lecturer to come to Mdina every other week than for the seminarians to commute between Valletta

[42] V. Borg, *The Seminary of Malta and the Ecclesiastical Benefices of the Maltese Islands* (Malta: St. Joseph's Home, 1965), p. 25.

[43] AIM Correspondence, vol. 90, p. 220.

[44] "... dovrà servire il Tribunale del S. Offizio nella medma isola sempre che sarà chiamato per interprete della lingua in Sac. Tribunale". AIM vol. 90, p. 23r.

[45] ʿAbd al-Raḥmān from Syria, a slave of the Order of St. John, was an interpreter. See AIM Ortensio, vol. 16, no. 5, p. 15r; Abū Salīm was called in 1603, see AIM Verallo, vol. 21, no. 26, p. 6v.

[46] AIM Correspondence, vol. 37 (ii), p. 318.

[47] A. Cremona, *art. cit.*, p. 11.

and Mdina almost daily. Dun Carbone accepted, doing his utmost to cope with the added duties, but hardly any time had gone by before he began to complain. He brought his case up with the Inquisitor Fabrizju Sarbelloni (1728-1731). The Inquisitor wrote to the Secretary of the Propaganda Fide, explaining the lecturer's difficulties. The Congregazione failed to reply and left Dun Carbone trudging along the Mdina road, as had previously been decided[48].

However, since the Congregazione did not come up with a solution, Dun Carbone decided to find one himself. As the seminarians had lost all interest in the study of the language and were not attending his lectures, he decided to stop going to Mdina altogether. Whether the seminarians were really uninterested in Arabic is highly questionable, as the failure could have been Dun Carbone's. He may have chosen the easiest way out, by not putting any effort into his teaching at Mdina in order to discourage his students, eliminating the need for him to go there. Whatever the case, one cannot ascertain why these lessons stopped. The Congregazione, on its part, denounced Dun Carbone for neglecting his duties and requested the Inquisition to start proceedings against him. The Inquisitor G.O.H. Manciforte Sperelli (1767-1771) presided over the trial in 1767. The bill of indictment against Dun Carbone presented by Cardinal Castelli, Prefect of the Congregazione de Propaganda Fide, also accused Dun Carbone of failing to award the prize of twenty Roman *scudi*, which was to be given annually to the best student of Arabic according to the original terms of the benefice "ta' l-Iskof", out of which the lecturer was paid. No details of this trial have been preserved except for Cremona's observations. He says that the Inquisitor was prejudiced in favour of Carbone, who in the end was acquitted of all charges. The case as presented by Dun Carbone denied that he had stopped teaching Arabic, as had been stated in the accusation against him, claiming he was still teaching at Valletta. The prize of twenty Roman *scudi* had ceased to be awarded because the students themselves would not bother even to sit for examinations. The Inquisitor himself admitted that Dun Girgor had always been of invaluable assistance whenever he needed him. According to the Inquisitor, Dun Girgor had helped the students of the Urban College when they were in Malta, had counselled many young people in their choice of a religious vocation, and had even provided financial help whenever they needed it.

[48] *Ibid.*

These arguments seemed to convince the Prefect of the Congregazione of Dun Carbone's innocence. He was pardoned the debt, amounting to three thousand Roman *scudi*, which the Congregazione was demanding from him. In one of his articles, Cremona goes on to say that Dun Carbonc had been indicted on false counts, but he refers to no document which confirms such a statement[49]. Such questions as what kind of trial this was, or who the witnesses were, will remain unanswered. All one can conclude is that the Inquisitor treated Carbone very leniently, on account of his generosity with the poor and his old age. Dun Girgor kept his post until he died in June 1773.

A few days later, the Inquisitor Antonion Lante (1771-1777) informed the Prefect of the Congregazione that the chair of Arabic was vacant. Interviews were held in Rome, and since this was not the usual practice, one begins to doubt how much the prefecture in Rome trusted the authorities in Malta. Dun Gużepp Calleja, one of the applicants, was appointed lecturer with duties specifying that he alternate on a weekly basis between Valletta and Mdina as had Dun Carbone[50]. A year or so later, even Dun Gużepp Calleja was finding it difficult to cope with his teaching duties at two separate places. He informed the Inquisitor of the academic and physical problems occasioned by this heavy travelling. Immediately, on July 4, 1774, the Inquisitor wrote to Cardinal Castelli, the Prefect of the Congregazione, suggesting that lectures should be held for a period of six months in Valletta and for another such period in Mdina, thus avoiding the need for unnecessary travel. This time the Congregazione accepted the Inquisitor's proposals. It concluded that one should abide by the opinion of the Inquisitor[51].

[49] A. Cremona, *art. cit.*, p. 12.
[50] A. Cremona, *art. cit.*, p. 27.
[51] *Ibid.*

Chapter II

THE TEACHING OF ARABIC AT THE UNIVERSITY OF MALTA

While Arabic was taught at Valletta and Mdina to religious and lay people without ever attaining any high standards, certain ecclesiastical authorities complained that this language had not been included in the list of academic subjects that could be read at the University of Malta, which was founded by Grandmaster Emmanuel Pinto de Fonseca (1741-1773) on November 22, 1769[1]. Grandmaster Manuel de Rohan Polduc (1775-1779) approved this suggestion, and immediately wrote to Pope Pius VI (1775-1799) to have the teaching of Arabic and the benefice "ta' l-Iskof" transferred to the university. The Pope ratified the Grandmaster's demands on September 20, 1795, and accordingly Arabic became part of the university curriculum, while the person entitled to the "ta' l-Iskof" benefice was promoted to the status of a university lecturer[2]. As a result of this, Dun Gużepp Calleja, the last lecturer at the school of Arabic that the Congregazione de Propaganda Fide had established as an institution in Malta, was the first to occupy the chair at the university[3]. Dun Calleja's career lasted twenty-five years, two years of which were spent at the university. He died at Tarxien, on May 19, 1798, at the time the French under Napoleon stood poised to invade Malta. Cesare Vassallo refers to Dun Gużepp Calleja as an archaeologist, a natural scientist, and a scholar of oriental languages, particularly Arabic. He also writes that a few months after his death, the soldiers who were then occupying Malta ransacked his house and looted his possessions, among which were a number of manuscripts[4].

The coming of Napoleon to Malta in 1798 began a new era in the history of the islands. The Knights of the Order of St. John under Ferdinand de Hompesch (1797-1798), the last grandmaster to rule Malta, were expelled after having been in power for two hundred and

[1] See extract from the decree, T. Zammit, *Malta* (Malta: A.C. Aquilina and Co., first published in 1948; third edition, 1971), p. 383.

[2] A. Cremona, *art. cit.*, p. 21.

[3] A. Cremona, *art. cit.*, pp. 30, 43. The institution has not died out; the benefice is still intact. The Church of Malta still receives the income from Għawdex. The Maltese diocese then sends this money to Rome. Cremona comments that it would be only fair and just if the benefice were to be of service to the Maltese.

[4] C. Vassallo, *Catalogo dei codici e manoscritti inediti* (Malta: 1856), no. 218.

sixty-eight years. The role of the Inquisition under the last Inquisitor, Giulio Carpegna (1793-1798), was also brought to an abrupt end. The University of Malta was closed by an order from Napoleon, who preferred establishing a central school to provide technical training rather than an education in the humanities. The teaching of French continued uninterrupted; although Arabic was considered important for political reasons, it was not taught, and the vacancy lasted four years.

During these four years, however, according to Cremona, Mikiel Anton Vassali (1764-1829) sent the Commissioner of the French Government a letter in which he requested to be appointed lecturer of Arabic, eligible for the income from the "ta' l-Iskof" benefice, which amounted to 1000 to 1200 French francs[5]. Vassalli's request was not granted during the entire French occupation[6].

All these events follow one another chronologically in the history of the teaching of Arabic in Malta. However, there were some conflicting incidents during the latter years which require some comment. According to Cremona, in 1788 Vassalli had been referred to by Simone Assemanno, Professor of the Arabic Language in Rome[7]. Ten years later, Professor Assemanno wrote to Professor O.G. Tychsen, telling him that Vassalli was a Professor of Oriental Languages and very well versed in Arabic[8].

The Congregazione had appointed Dun Gużepp Calleja lecturer at its school. Later he was automatically promoted to a university post. There is no record that Vassalli had been made lecturer during the time Dun Calleja was holding his chair at the University. On the other hand, one cannot conclude that Vassalli bestowed upon himself the title of Professor without having ever taught at the university. That he knew Arabic is unquestionable; his works prove this.

Probably, Vassalli studied Arabic under Dun Gużepp Calleja at the Mdina Seminary between 1780 and 1787. He believed that a scholar could not become erudite in the study of the Maltese language without first mastering Arabic, as the two languages are closely related. For this reason, he went to Rome to continue his studies of Semitic languages, particularly Arabic[9].

[5] A. Cremona, *art. cit.*, p. 14.

[6] *Ibid.*

[7] A. Cremona, *Mikiel Anton Vassalli u Żminijietu*, p. 93.

[8] *Ibid.*

[9] For more details about Vassalli, see D. Marshall, *History of the Maltese Language in Local Education* (Malta: University Press, 1971), pp. 8, 9.

The Congregazione was still responsible for choosing a lecturer of Arabic, and the University of Malta accepted its decisions in this regard. In 1802, after the death of Dun Gużepp Calleja, the Congregazione held examinations for selecting a new lecturer. Fra Ġużeppi Grassi, a Maltese Chaplain of the Order of St. John, took this examination and reached the required level, but because of serious problems that had arisen between Rome and Malta, he was apparently not appointed. Consequently he never received any income from the "ta' l-Iskof" benefice[10].

When the British took Malta over from the French, Captain Alexander Ball (1799-1801) reopened the university and without consulting the Congregazione, appointed Antonio Faḍl Allāh Professor of Arabic[11]. This post had not been filled for almost five years. But after less than three months, the Professor, who was being paid sixty *scudi* by the treasury, decided for some reason to resign. Once again the chair was vacant.

During Faḍl Allāh's term of appointment, Fra. Grassi was sent to Tunisia by Ball himself to study the local dialect[12]. Meanwhile, in 1803, Rear-Admiral Sir Alexander Ball wrote to Cardinal Consalvi, Secretary for the Papal States, requesting that the salary of the Arabic lectorate be discussed and that Fra. Ġużeppi Grassi be given the post[13]. The Congregazione, on its part, abstained from a decision, and Grassi was not given his appointment.

The Congregazione refused Grassi the right to be paid out of the "ta' l-Iskof" benefice, which ultimately depended upon the labour of the Maltese and Gozitan farmers. Perhaps Rome saw no reason why a lecturer should be appointed when there might be no interest at all in the language. On the other hand, Rome may simply have mistrusted the British system. Further, since the number of Maltese missionary fathers had declined in that century, and since the benefice had been established for the exclusive help of the missions, the income derived from it could have been directed to the Urban College of the Propaganda Fide in Rome[14], rather than made available to the lecturer of Arabic in Malta.

[10] A. Cremona, *art. cit.*, p. 15.

[11] NLM Archivio Tesoro B. vol. 182, no. 312, pp. 217, 223; AUM Acta Melitensis (1798-1809), p. 48.

[12] A. Cremona, *art. cit.*, p. 15. Cremona comments that Faḍl Allāh is an Arabic name, in spite of the fact that the university register lists his as Armenian. But Cremona seems to have forgotten that many Armenians adopted Arabic names in Arab countries.

[13] V. Azzopardi, *op. cit.*, p. 141.

[14] G. Scerri, *op. cit.*, p. 59.

While Malta and Rome were involved in discussions over this benefice, Commissioner Ball decided that Patri Anastasio, a Franciscan, should teach Classical Arabic at the university[15]. He held this appointment for only two years; according to the necrology of the Franciscan Province in Malta; he died on August 20, 1807.

On October 3, 1807 Grassi, after this long delay, was given the lectureship[16]. His salary, issued by the Government Treasurer, amounted to two pounds sterling, one shilling, and eight pence[17].

During the time Grassi was teaching Arabic, Hookham Frère, after an active career with the Foreign Office, retired in Malta in 1821. He started translating a few works from Latin and Greek, and encouraged many Maltese to adopt a scholarly and scientific attitude in the study of their own language and Arabic[18]. But the most relevant of all his achievements was that he began creating an interest in Arabic in primary schools[19].

Interest was gradually increasing when on December 27, 1824, Frederick Hankey (1824-1837), the first Secretary of State in Malta, informed the Treasurer that the salary previously paid to the lecturer of Arabic must henceforth be paid to the secretary of the university[20]. This meant that Grassi would not receive any salary at all. One can readily understand what motivated Hankey to take such a decision; most probably he learned about the salary derived from the benefice and concluded that the problem was properly the concern of the Bishop of Malta, Ferdinandu Mattei (1807-1831)[21], and not the Treasurer of the British Administration. A few days later, the Bishop replied that although the benefice had been founded in Malta it was under the control of the Congregazione, which was fully responsible for it and which directed all funds to where they were most needed. For this reason, such funds were to be forwarded directly to Rome[22].

During both the French occupation and British rule, all efforts to utilise this benefice in the best interests of the Maltese were fruitless. Malta had no say in the management of its own affairs, which in this

[15] FPAM Miscellanea B., p. 27.

[16] NLM Acta Academiae Melitensis (1836-1839).

[17] A. Cremona, *art. cit.*, p. 16.

[18] D. Marshall, *op. cit.*, p. 7.

[19] *Ibid.*

[20] About Hankey and his government service, see H.J. Lee, *Malta 1813-1914* (Malta: Progress Press, 1972), pp. 51, 52.

[21] AUM Government Letters (1823-1832) (unpaginated).

[22] A. Cremona, *art. cit.*, p. 16.

case were dictated from Rome. The local ecclesiastical authorities occasionally tried to prevail upon the Congregazione, but the instances when they were successful were rare indeed. Whether they were not sufficiently influential in the higher bureaucratic circles in Rome, or were reluctant to uphold the rights of the Maltese, owing to their weakness, is hard to say. But whatever the reason, this case illustrates the ecclesiastical colonialism to which the Church of Malta was subject.

The teaching of Arabic was then adopting a more secular outlook. At university level, it fostered an interest more academic in spirit, while the original missionary purpose ceased to exist. Arabic was being taught purely for its own sake, as an end in itself. As well, it was considered an important subject for study as a language that had exerted great influence on the Maltese dialect.

Grassi's teaching career at the university lasted until 1838, when he was made redundant owing to certain changes that were implemented[23]. According to notes entered in his manuscripts, he used to teach also at the Lyceum[24], although Arabic had apparently not been introduced there before 1838, the year Grassi retired from his university post. A report on education, published in 1838 by John Austin and George Cornewall Lewis, comments on the necessity of teaching Arabic at the Lyceum and on the importance of the integration of this subject into the curriculum[25]. However, one cannot ignore the possibility that this subject could have been taught at the Lyceum prior to 1838 on an irregular and unofficial basis. Academically, the Lyceum had always been related to the University of Malta, and since the need for Arabic had long been felt, it may have been introduced at the Lyceum to provide preliminary training for university courses[26].

On the other hand, the teaching of Arabic in primary schools had been established, following the encouragement and advice given by Hookham Frère[27]. Bus as yet, no reliable document has provided information regarding the number of teachers employed for this purpose in these schools. We know, though, that its scope needed to be expanded and improved[28]. We also know that all aspects of elementary education fell under the jurisdiciton of the University Rectorate[29].

[23] AUM Letter Book (1836-1838); Government Letters (1823-1838) (unpaginated).

[24] NLM MS 516 (frontispiece).

[25] Report of the Royal Commission 1836-39: "The Lyceum".

[26] A.V. Laferla, *British Malta*, vol. 2 (Malta: 1947), p. 33.

[27] See Austin and Lewis, Report on the institutions for public instruction (April 27, 1838). Letters of the Colonial Office, Office of Public Documents (London), 158/116.

[28] NLM MS 263, Document 9.

[29] *Ibid.*

Between 1836 and 1839, many efforts were made to reform the educational system in Malta. But although the elementary schools were going through many changes intended to increase and advance knowledge[30], the university was experiencing radical reforms which curtailed the number of professors while increasing the salaries of the few who continued to hold their posts. In spite of this, the ultimate result was an upgrading of university standards[31].

These academic and financial reforms at the university prompt some personal comments and conclusions. As an institution, the university intended to reassess its academic levels and amend its curricula. Keenan, the British Government representative who had been commissioned to draw up a report on education in Malta, remarked that the study of oriental languages at the university deserved full support, and that he could not understand why a professor had not yet been appointed[32]. As far as I can conclude, when Grassi held the Chair of Arabic he was not so influential, having failed to elicit the expected response from his students and the general public. This might have been due to the influence of the Italophiles, who favoured the Italian language and culture and looked down upon Arabic.

The university authorities decided to abolish Arabic from their oriental languages, although in fact, only two had been taught: Hebrew and Arabic[33]. This step could have been taken for any of several reasons. But Keenan's proposition, that Arabic should be included in the list of options offered to students for their specialization in the Faculty of Arts, never materialised.

The British officials, after studies and research carried out on the island, made realistic and objective suggestions to the Government of Malta regarding education. John Austin, George Cornewall, and P.J. Keenan all felt the need for the study of Arabic in Malta; but the British commissioners were restricted by financial limitations on the one hand and on the other by the prejudiced advice of both lay and ecclesiastical authorities, most of whom were Italophiles. Nevertheless, when Hookham Frère was in Malta in 1821, through the encouragement and support he gave, he succeeded in persuading a number of Maltese teachers to teach Arabic. The primary school at Żejtun was

[30] Bouverie to Glenelg (September 4, 1838), no. 103. Letters of the Colonial Office, 158/102.

[31] Glenelg to Bouverie (July 20, 1838), no. 267. Letters of the Colonial Office, 159/17.

[32] P.J. Keenan, *Report on the Educational System in Malta* (Dublin: 1879), p. 57.

[33] *Ibid.*

one of the first to introduce Arabic into its programme, which consisted of religious doctrine and Maltese[34].

The Żejtun Primary School was opened in 1819 under the administration of Dun Bert Sant, a diocesan priest. (As I have already pointed out, schools at that time were run by the ecclesiastical authorities). Dun Alwiġ Camilleri, a parish priest from Ħal Għargħur, was authorised by Bishop Ferdinandu Mattei (1807-1831) to succeed Dun Bert. Dun Camilleri introduced the teaching of Classical Arabic in his school, but we are not certain when[35]. According to Keenan, there were between thirty and forty pupils attending. Through Reverend Schlienz, an active Protestant missionary in Malta, we come to know that Keenan, on a visit to this school, decided to determine the level of the pupils' proficiency in Classical Arabic. He noted that the pupils were well trained, and even knew how to read excerpts from the Scriptures[36]. He emerged satisfied, and in his personal notes, wrote that if the school had had a competent teacher, adequate textbooks, and all the necessary supplies, it would have been among the best on the islands[37].

There are no records revealing the identity of this teacher; however, we do know that Dun Alwiġ Camilleri was a dedicated teacher of Maltese. The preface to a nineteenth century reader in Maltese provides ample proof of this[38]. Still, it is doubtful whether he himself taught Arabic, or whether he employed somebody else for this purpose.

In 1838, after the completion of the Keenan Report, the government decided to assume responsibility for the educational system in Malta. This meant that the Żejtun School was to become a public school. The Church did not contest this issue, and government took over. The result was that the teaching of Arabic stopped[39]. Three factors may have caused this: firstly, the government may have shown a lack of interest in the teaching of Arabic owing to financial exigencies, as had been the case with the university when the teaching of Arabic was abolished despite reports advising the improvement of the existing course. Secondly, Dun Alwiġ may have decided to resign from his teaching post once the schools were nationalised. Thirdly, interest in the lan-

[34] E.B. Vella, *Storja taz-Żejtun u Marsaxlokk* (Malta, s.d.), Part 3.

[35] The Keenan Report (1838), p. 77.

[36] C.F. Schlienz, *Views on the Improvement of the Maltese Language and its Use for the Purposes of Education and Literature* (Malta, 1838), p. 57.

[37] *Ibid.*

[38] F. Vella — G. Montebello Pulis, *Chtieb Ilkari yau Dahla ghall Ilsien Malti* (Livorno, 1824).

[39] E.B. Vella, *op. cit.*, Section 3.

guage may have declined, and consequently the government, heeding complaints made by the Italophiles against the teaching of Arabic, decided to abolish it altogether in preference to more essential subjects in the curriculum.

The teaching of Arabic continued at the lyceum and in Valletta. It seems that in 1838 Grassi lost both his university and lyceum posts. In his stead, the British Government appointed Aḥmad Fāris al-Shidyāq, an Arab from Lebanon, who was employed as an assistant at the Arabic press located on 138 Strada San Cristoforo, Valletta[40]. Cremona writes that Shidyāq was appointed lecturer on December 22, immediately after Grassi's termination of employment[41]. This appointment cannot be verified, because there is no reference made to Shidyāq in the records of the university, even though Shidyāq himself professed to be a lecturer at this institution[42]. It is certain, however, that Shidyāq taught at the lyceum and at the Valleta Government School. His appointment, issued by the colonial government, defining his post as lecturer at the lyceum and the elementary school carried an annual salary of fifty pounds sterling. This income was unconnected with what he earned at the Arabic press. Shidyāq frequently went to London. He was engaged in translating the Holy Scriptures under the direction of the Society for Promoting Christian Knowledge, together with the Arabists Thomas Jarrett and Thomas Robinson[43].

This activity took most of his time, hence his career as a lecturer, while possibly fruitful, did not last long. On October 24, 1850, after having been away in London for two years, he informed the colonial government that he did not intend to return to Malta. Effectively, then, his career ended in 1848[44].

Judging by the publications to which he contributed while working at the Arabic press, Shidyāq appears to have been very competent. On the other hand, it is difficult for one to come to the same conclusion regarding his teaching. Neither can one say how disposed or receptive his students were. However, a reference must be made here to a remark passed during the university council meeting on April 12, 1839: the rector admitted that, contrary to their expectations, the students had

[40] The Arabic printing press in Malta started to function in 1821.

[41] A. Cremona, *art. cit.*, p. 17.

[42] P. Cachia, "An Arab's view of 19th century Malta, from Shidyaq's 'Al-Wāṣiṭah li-Maʿrifat Aḥwāl Māliṭah' ", *Maltese Folklore Review*, I, i (1962): 32.

[43] A.J. Arberry, "Fresh Light on Ahmad Faris al-Shidyaq", *Islamic Culture*, 26, i (1952): 164.

[44] A. Cremona, *art. cit.*, p. 17.

lost all their former enthusiasm for the study of Arabic and Hebrew[45]. Which students was the rector referring to: those at the university, those at the lyceum, or both? If he meant the university students, as most probably he did since Hebrew was only taught there, Aḥmad Fāris al-Shidyāq must have been teaching at the university, as he himself claimed.

Three years after Shidyāq resigned from his teaching duties at the lyceum and the elementary school, Robertu Casolani began teaching Arabic at the lyceum and the university. Two months later, Casolani left the island, and Gejtanu Ciancio was given a *pro tempore* appointment from June 23, 1853 to September 23, 1858[46]. On september 10, 1858, Casolani sent the Assistant Secretary of the British Government in Malta a letter from Istanbul, in which he stated that he could not return to his teaching duties in Malta. Consequently, the teaching of Arabic remained under the charge of Gejtanu Ciancio.

Officially a Professor of Arabic and Oriental Languages, Casolani had a salary amounting to one hundred twenty pounds sterling; we are not certain of Ciancio's salary, though his appointment included teaching both at the lyceum and at the university, as had been the case with Casolani[47].

In 1881, Casolani was reinstated in his teaching post, which he continued to hold until 1889. We do not know the exact date of Casolani's return to Malta, or whether Casolani himself asked the Government to reinstate him in the post he formerly held in 1853. Based on the Keenan Report, dated 1879, we may infer that the Arabic lessons at the lyceum (taught, in those days, by Ciancio) were poorly attended and that the class of only thirteen students was disorganised[48].

At the end of Casolani's appointment in 1889, Antonio Sarreo was assigned to teach Arabic at the lyceum only. Arabic as a language was losing its appeal; public opinion favoured cultivating and developing the Maltese language, which at that time had just gone through a difficult phase of conflict between Italophiles and Arabophiles (those who supported the Arabic language and culture). Both parties produced convincing arguments to the general public in Malta, and found adherents among Maltese, Italians, and English alike. The Italophiles suggested that Maltese should be adapted to the Italian alphabet and

[45] NLM Readings of the University General Council (April 12, 1839).
[46] A. Cremona, *art. cit.*, p. 18.
[47] *Ibid.*
[48] P.J. Keenan, *art. cit.*, p. 57, Section 51.

phonetics in orthographic matters, while the Arabophiles on their part held that Maltese, being a Semitic language and an Arabic dialect, should be adapted to Arabic[49].

The last lecturer of Arabic in Malta was Reverend Yūsuf Sebhlani, a Maronite diocesan priest from Lebanon, whose term of appointment lasted from 1895 to 1914/15. Like his predecessor, he was assigned to lecture only at the lyceum. The presence of a Maronite in Malta was of great interest indeed, but we do not know anything about what happened between 1889 and 1895, nor what turns the teaching of Arabic took after 1895. The arrival of Sebhlani aroused a certain interest in the study of oriental history, especially those aspects which concerned the Maronite rite throughout the ages. Regarding the study of Arabic, one must point out that two of the greatest Maltese scholars and writers, Temi Zammit and Robertu Mifsud Bonnici, studied Arabic under Sebhlani. By 1914/15, the colonial government no longer saw a need for the lyceum Arabic class, firstly because the attendance had declined drastically, and secondly because the government was then on a very tight budget, since Britain had already become involved in the World War. In this manner, the teaching of Arabic in the Maltese Islands came to an end.

SUMMARY AND CONCLUSION

Officially, the teaching of Arabic in Malta began in 1632 and ended in 1914/15. Its purpose was twofold: (a) religious, to assist missionaries bound for Arab countries, and (b) academic, to help Maltese scholars trace the development of their language back to its Arabic roots. For the success of this study, a benefice, referred to as "ta' l-Iskof", was founded in the early years to provide for the salary of the lecturer. Both the benefice and the lectorate were subject to the approval of the Congregazione de Propaganda Fide. Many disputes between Malta and Rome resulted in bitter controversies. Later, the benefice passed under the university administration, and continued to provide the lecturer's

[49] J. Aquilina, *Papers in Maltese Linguistics* (Malta: Progress Press, first edition 1961; Malta University Press, 1970), pp. 80, 81. I disagree with Aquilina's statement: "Thank heavens the Arabists did not have it their way, for their system certainly would have cut us off from the literature of the countries where the Latin script is used". Scripts are no barriers as much as languages and cultures are. Fārisi is an Indoeuropean language and Arabic is a Semitic language; both written in Arabic script, yet, both languages and cultures (to a lesser extent) are distant from each other.

salary. While the lectorate of Arabic reached high academic standards, problems continued to multiply, until the benefice was finally separated from the university. Although rents pertaining to the benefice were collected (as they still are) from Maltese and Gozitan farmers, they were sent to the Urban College of the Propaganda Fide.

A solution was found as to how the lecturer of Arabic was to be paid. But during the reform of the educational system in Malta, certain changes occurred which evidently abolished the lectorate from the university. Thereafter Arabic continued to be taught only at the lyceum and in elementary schools. Towards the end of the nineteenth century, the public lost interest in Arabic, as it began to realise the importance of its own language, which was gradually gaining some stability with an orthography of its own. The study of Arabic in Malta ended during the first year of World War I, in 1914/15.

Chapter III

ARABIC WORKS IN LANGUAGE AND CULTURE

(a) The First Collections of Oriental Manuscripts

During the early years of the fifteenth century, there arose an interest in collecting oriental manuscripts in the Vatican, which felt the need to amass a wealth of literature from the East and become familiar with it. One of its motives was to understand the technique and philosophy of the archenemy of Christianity at a time when the Ottoman Empire was assuming dominance throughout Europe and the Mediterranean, even threatening the religious authorities in the Vatican.

The Christian Churches of the East were also threatened, although in this case, the real trouble originated not from the political policies of the Muslim Ottoman Turks, but from the political-religious controversies between the Christians and the Vatican. To settle such disputes and safeguard peace and unity in the Catholic Church, the Vatican sent political and religious mediators. One of these was a Maltese, Leonardu Abela (1541-1605), better known as Abel[1]. He was born at Mdina and studied in Malta, where he graduated as a doctor of canon and civil Law. Around 1578, he went to Rome and in 1582 was appointed capitular vicar and Bishop of Sidon in the Middle East, with a brief from Pope Gregory XIII (1572-1583)[2]. During his four-year stay in Rome, Abel was appointed interpreter and confessor of Arabic[3].

Although it is questionable whether Abel studied Arabic in Malta or Rome, his commentaries on a number of the Arabic manuscripts he brought from the East indicate that he was more than interested in the language and, indeed, seems to have been fluent in it.

Whatever his motives for studying Arabic, and whatever his linguistic facilities as a Maltese may have been, Abel was appointed mediator to

[1] G. Levi della Vida, *Ricerche sulla formazione del piu antico dei manoscritti orientali della biblioteca vaticana* (Vatican: Biblioteca Apostolica Vaticana, 1939), p. 200; bibliographies on Abela, see G.F. Abela, *Malta illustrata* (Malta: 1647); I.S. Mifsud, *Biblioteca maltese* (Malta: 1764), pp. 38-46. According to L. Cheikho, the renowned Abela family in Beirut is related to this bishop. See *Al-Mashriq*, 6 (1903): 254-265.

[2] R. Mifsud Bonnici, *Dizzjunarju Bijo-Bibljografiku Nazzjonali* (Malta: Department of Information, 1960), p. 2.

[3] G. Levi della Vida, *op. cit.*, p. 201. He wrote that Abela's mother tongue was Maltese and this helped him to speak Arabic fluently. An interesting comment!

the Levant to unite the Jacobites with the Vatican. On March 12, 1583, he went to Aleppo. He was well suited for such a mission, where he would be dealing with Christians whose culture was completely different from the Latin one prevalent in the Vatican. With Abel to bridge the gap between these two cultures, the Arabic and the Latin, it was felt the mission was assured of success[4].

Unfortunately, the mission failed. Abel's visit to the Levant might have left a breach in the unity of the Church, with perhaps even some undesirable consequences for the Catholic Church; nonetheless, it had its own merits. Wherever he went, Abel managed to collect a vast number of manuscripts in Syriac, Arabic, Persian, and Armenian from various monasteries, convents, and churches. Abel studied them carefully and wrote his comments on them in Latin[5].

The manuscripts are all sixteenth century; most were found in Syria. He carefully copied a number of others that he was unable to take to Rome[6]. Some of them are rare and valuable, as they give important cultural and linguistic insight into the Oriental Churches.

Apart from his apostolic work, Abel apparently spent some time writing a grammar of Arabic and some notes about the teaching of the Chaldean language[7]. It is doubtful, though, whether he undertook such academic work during his early years in Rome, when he was appointed mediator, or towards the end of his life. Ġan Franġisk Abela (1582-1655), a historiographer, made direct reference to these manuscripts, but as they are not listed in any library, either in Rome or in Malta, one concludes that either Abela must have seen them while they were still in the possession of Bishop Leonardu Abela, or after they had formed part of some collection in Rome or Malta[8].

Bishop Abela died on May 12, 1605 in Rome, where he was buried in the Basilica di San Giovanni Laterano. Some years after his death, the Vatican acquired a vast collection of Islamic manuscripts. These were donated by the Knights of Malta, who had taken them as booty from galleys that they raided to capture Muslim slaves[9].

[4] *Ibid.*

[5] *Ibid.*, pp. 222-257. The number of manuscripts is 110, but according to Levi della Vida, it is doubtful whether twenty-eight of them ever formed part of Abela's collection.

[6] G. Levi della Vida, *op. cit.*, p. 255.

[7] According to what G.F. Abela wrote in *Malta illustrata*; see R. Mifsud Bonnici, *op. cit.*, p. 3; A. Cremona, *Mikiel Anton Vassali*, p. 9.

[8] G.F. Abela was related to Leonardu Abela. Perhaps Leonardu Abela had spoken of these manuscripts, and G.F. Abela heard of them, but they were never written.

[9] G. Levi della Vida, *op. cit.*, p. 260.

Furthermore, in 1609, Monsignor Leonetto della Corbara, Apostolic Delegate and General Visitor of the Island of Malta (1607-1609), transferred fifteen manuscripts from the library of the Inquisition in Malta to the Vatican library, as he had been directed to do by Scipione Borghese, nephew of Pope Paul V (1609-1618)[10].

Corbara's collection is not of any particular importance nor academic value. If these books had been looted from Ottoman galleys by the Knights of Malta, the probability is that they would not have been important; no Muslim would have dared to carry, without good reason, anything valuable with him on his travels through the Mediterranean, infested as it was with pirates.

This collection includes many extracts from the Qur'ān, prayers, magic, and some romance writings. While the religious texts were intended to provide spiritual comfort, the romances were for light reading. Most probably these books[11] had been captured from Ottoman galleys prior to 1609[12]. It is indeed a small collection, and it is strange that only two manuscripts were codified in the Vatican, considering the great number of slaves that were usually kept in Malta. The two manuscripts in the Vatican are: one (MS Turc. 8) consisting of common prayers in Turkish, donated by Cardinal San Giorgio di Malta on March 2, 1600; the other (MS Turc. 17), *Mewlid el-Nebi* by Süleymân Çelebi, donated in 1686 most probably by the same Cardinal[13]. The latter, written in Turkish, is about the birth of the prophet Muḥammad.

(b) Early Arabic Linguistic Works

In Europe, the first Arabic grammar to be written scientifically was that by the scholar Thomas Erpenius. It was published in Leiden in 1613 (8 vo, 124 pp.)[14]. In 1617, Erpenius, who taught Arabic at the University of Leiden, published another Arabic grammar, accompanied by his

[10] B. dal Pozzo, *Historia della sacra religione militare di San Giovanni gerosolmitano detta di Malta* vol. I, (Verona: 1703), pp. 536, 552. At the Cathedral Archives, Mdina, a note refers to twelve books in Arabic (and Turkish) at the Library of the Inquisition. See AIM Carbonesio, vol. 33, no. 383.

[11] P.M. Baumgarten, in his book *Neue Kunde von Alten Bibeln*, Vol. 2 (Roma: 1922), p. 152, was concerned about the collection that was taken to Rome from Malta.

[12] Dal Pozzo refers to the tough and troubled period prior to 1609, *op. cit.*, pp. 521-546; E. Rossi, *Storia della marina dell' Ordine di San Giovanni di Gerusalemme, di Rodi e di Malta* (Roma: 1926), pp. 61-62.

[13] In the latter, a note says: "Dell' Illmo sig. Car(dina)le San Giorgio", but there is no reference that he came from Malta. Levi della Vida thinks otherwise, see p. 263.

[14] *Philologia Orientalis* (Leiden: E.J. Brill, 1976), p. 63.

comments in Latin. The grammar was modelled on the *Ājurrūmiyya*. It is all vocalised, as in 1592 there had already been a publication from the Medicean Press which had not been treated in this manner[15].

Obicini's grammar, published in Rome in 1631, was to a certain extent written to Erpenius' model. Tomaso Obicini, a Franciscan, followed the *Ājurrūmiyya* very closely and, like Erpenius, wrote all his comments in Latin. In 1622 Obicini, authorised by a decree from the Propaganda Fide[16], founded the College of San Pietro de Montario in Rome. According to Lantschoot, he was well versed in the oriental languages — Hebrew, Syriac, and Chaldean[17].

Ājurrūmiyya was the Arabic grammar written by Abū ʿAlī Muḥammad b. Muḥammad b. Dāūd al-Ṣinhājī b. Ājurrūm, who taught at Fās and died in 1323. This concise book is written in a very simple style[18]. It was taken to Europe about three hundred years after the death of the author and translated into Latin, which was the academic language in universities all over Europe. This book is still to be found in most countries throughout the world, and in some Arab countries, it remains the standard textbook used in the teaching of Arabic[19].

Obicini's grammar was taken to Malta and today forms part of the Franciscan Provincial Library at Valletta. This library holds the greatest collection of Arabic manuscripts on the island, as the Franciscans had always been in the forefront in introducing and organising the teaching of this language. Indeed, it was Franġisk Flieles who dedicated all his time and energy to studying Arabic and building this library.

Patri Flieles had bought a Muslim slave from the Order of St. John to help him in his studies and duties as a lecturer of Arabic[20]. The slave, ʿAlī b. Yaḥyā 'l-Zawāwī, copied a great number of Arabic manuscripts for Flieles; his handwriting was very clear and legible. He

[15] C. De Schurrer, *Bibliotheca Arabica* (Amsterdam: Oriental Press, 1968), p. 23.

[16] A. Kleinhans, *op. cit.*, pp. 10, 14; see also J. Th. Zenker, *Bibliotheca Orientalis* (Leipzig: 1846), p. 18.

[17] A. van Lantschoot, "Lettre inéditée de Thomas Obicini à Pietro della Valle", *Rivista degli Studi Orientali*, 28 (1953): 118-129.

[18] The author of this book translated the *Ājurrūmiyya* into English, adding some remarks on a number of grammatical points. See D. Agius, "A Study of the *Kitāb al-Ājurrūmiyya* as a Manual of Arabic Linguistics", M.A. Dissertation, University of Toronto, 1977.

[19] C. Brockelmann, *Geschichte der Arabischen Litteratur*, Vol. 2 (Leiden: E. J. Brill, 1949), p. 308. The author does not refer to the MS Collection of the *Ājurrūmiyya* in Malta.

[20] E. Rossi, *art. cit.*, pp. 4, 5; G. Scerri, *op. cit.*, pp. 50-66.

made use of Biblical texts to derive a number of his grammatical comments[21]. Al-Zawāwī, beyond doubt, was the only slave in Malta who managed to contribute so much to the writing of Arabic on the island. According to the manuscripts kept at the Franciscan Library, he was employed at the convent between 1629 and 1633. (see illustration 1)

Pieces of information scattered throughout the manuscripts copied by al-Zawāwī throw some light on the identity of this slave and his relations with his master. Al-Zawāwī, an old man[22], referred to his master as "a man, much respected and intelligent; a man who is of such great help to slaves"[23]. He was evidently well-treated by Flieles and quite content with his work[24]. Al-Zawāwī did not feel competent enough to write everything which had been requested of him by Patri Flieles, yet he understood that his writings were to be of importance to his master and the students[25].

In the nineteenth century, the *Ājurrūmiyya* was apparently no longer used in Malta, which was then going through its richest phase in the history of Arabic studies, owing to the enormous revival of interest in the language. Ġużeppi Grassi's Arabic grammar, which was an Italian translation from a Latin original, was being used instead. The Latin text had been written in 1687 by Fra Agapito A Valle, a lecturer of Arabic in Padova, about fifty years after Obicini had published his grammar and seventy years after that of Erpenius. In the introduction to Grassi's grammar, there is an interesting illustration of a human head: along the line of the cranium, neck, chin, and mouth are the two words *al-lugha* ("the language") and *al-ʿarabiyya* ("Arabic"). The latter forms part of the throat with the letter /ع/. An eye forms the word *naḥw* ("grammar"); the illustration suggests one who observes whatever one sees. Along the back of the head and further down towards the ears, there appears the date the manuscript was written, 1868.

Apart from Flieles and Grassi, there was another Maltese who contributed a great deal to the cause of Arabic in Malta. This was Patri Pawlu Deguara, a Franciscan from Mosta (1809-1888). According to documents found at the Franciscan Provincial Library in Valletta, Deguara was a zealous missionary who was much talented in Arabic.

21 MSS A8, A11, A14.
22 MS A16, p. 54r.
23 *Ibid.*
24 MS Al, p. 77v.
25 MS A12, p. 114r.

On February 19, 1839[26] he left Malta and went to the Levant where he visited Latakiyya, Jerusalem, Bethlehem, Alexandria, and Cairo. He even travelled to Tripoli, Libya. This extended experience of almost fifteen years in Arab countries developed in him considerable capability in the Arabic language and culture. Patri Deguara is said to have taught Arabic in Bethlehem[27].

The manuscripts at the Franciscan Provincial Library indicate that Deguara dedicated himself to the teaching of Arabic and to the writing of an Arabic dictionary[28]. Grassi was also compiling an Arabic-Italian dictionary of 2211 pages during this period[29], although there is no record of any date. Deguara also compiled another Italian-Arabic dictionary consisting of verbs, to which he added a list of common expressions and conversational passages from everyday life[30].

In the nineteenth century, the Christian Missionary Society set up an Arabic press at 138 Strada San Cristoforo, Valletta[31]. This was a period of intense activity because, as the press had been transferred to Malta from Beirut during political tensions between the Maronite and Protestant Churches which began in 1815, Malta became the centre of Protestant religious activities. The Arabic press, together with others including the Greek, Hebrew, Italian, and Armenian-Turkish presses[32], became the means for the propagation of Protestant doctrine.

During the early 1830's, the American mission invited a Maronite from Lebanon, Aḥmad Fāris al-Shidyāq (1804-1887), to Malta, employing him at the press as a translator[33]. Shidyāq was also appointed lecturer of Arabic at the university and the lyceum.

Shidyāq's literary activities can be traced to the period he spent under the guidance of prominent professors in Egypt. He continued writing in Malta and his literary style showed during this period excellent qualities. He evidently dealt with every Arabic publication

[26] FPAM, Decretum Sacra Congregazione di Propaganda Fide (s.d.), vol. 14, document 65.

[27] Status Descriptivus Custodia Terra Sancta, p. 97; see the certificate of Bernardinus Montefranco, Custodian of the Holy Land; FPAM, s.d., vol. 14, document 88.

[28] FPAM, MSS A20 (i and ii).

[29] NLM, MS 516.

[30] FPAM, MSS A18, A19.

[31] J. Zaydan, *Tā'rīkh Ādāb al-Lughat al-'Arabiyya*, Vol. 4 (Cairo: Dār al-Hilāl, 1957), p. 45.

[32] Margaret T. Hills, "Languages of the Near East 1831-1860", MS. American Bible Society, Missionary Research Library, New York, 1964; section III-F, p. 68.

[33] A. Cremona, *art. cit.*, pp. 16, 17, f.n. 23, 24.

issued by the press[34] Shidyāq himself published *Al-Bākūrāt al-Shahiyya* (1836, later published in Istanbul in 1881/82), an English grammar written in Arabic. He also published Jirmānūs Farḥat's (d. 1732) Arabic grammar, *Baḥth al-Maṭālib* (1836). As for prose, he published *Al-Lafīf li-Kull Ma'nā Ẓarīf* (1839), an elementary Arabic reader. A year later he published *Kitāb al-Muḥāwara* (1840), a grammar workbook consisting of exercises in Arabic and English, accompanied by familiar conversational extracts. During his stay in Malta, he also wrote a *qaṣīda*, a poem in honour of the Beğ of Tunis, but it seems that this was never published by the Arabic press[35].

Shidyāq had been employed mainly to help in the translation of the Bible under the direction of the Anglo-American Mission. Such religious and literary activity would not have been possible without the help of the two Arabists Thomas Jarrett and Thomas Robinson[36].

(c) Arabic Literary Works by Maltese Authors

One of the first Maltese to make a comprehensive study of Arabic was the Franciscan Patri Ludwig Muscat (1571-1635). He was one of the foremost writers of his time, and in 1622, the Sacra Congregazione nominated him and Tomaso Obicini to establish Arabic studies at the College of the Propaganda Fide[37]. Interest in such studies had already become popular in certain parts of Europe, most particularly in Holland; in Rome, the Medici Press was established in 1584 through the insistence of Pope Gregory XIII (1572-1585). Moreover, between 1590 and 1610, the scholar Giovanni Battista Raimondi published eight books in Arabic through another press which he had set up on his own[38].

In 1629, Patri Muscat succeeded Obicini as lecturer of Arabic at the College of the Propaganda Fide when the latter retired from his post. He also spent some time in Spain, where he was commissioned by King Philip IV (1621-1665) to translate some Arabic manuscripts into

[34] E. Stock, *The History of the Church Missionary Society*, Vol. 1 (London: 1899), p. 219.

[35] H.L. Fleischer, "Eine newarabische Kaside", *Zeitschrift der Deutschen Morgenlandischen Gesellschaft*, 5 (1851): 249-257.

[36] A.J. Arberry, "Fresh Light on Ahmad Faris al-Shidyaq", *Islamic Culture*, 26, i (1852): 164.

[37] A. Kleinhans, *op. cit.*, p. 370.

[38] J. Fück, "Geschichte der Semitischen Sprachwissenschaft", *Semitistik-Handbuch der Orientalistik*, Vol. 3 (Leiden: E. J. Brill, 1954), pp. 53-56.

Spanish[39]. The Spanish Inquisitor was greatly impressed by the extraordinary talent Muscat showed, requesting him to remain in Spain as advisor to the Supreme Tribunal[40]. For some reason, Muscat refused the offer, and in 1634 returned to Sicily where a year later he died, aged sixty-four. His numerous works in Arabic and Italian[41] are now part of the Vatican Library[42].

Dun Domenico Magri (1604-1672) is referred to by Cremona as having translated the *Kitāb Nuzhat al-Mushtāq fī Dhikr al-Amṣār wa 'l-Aqṭār wa 'l-Buldān wa 'l-Madā'in wa 'l-Āfāq* by al-Idrīsī (d. 1154) from Arabic into Latin in 1626[43]. This work, which is also known as *Kitāb Rujār*, is a geographical study written by Idrīsī in 1154 when he was employed at the palace of King Roger II of Sicily (1111-1154).

However, Magri and his work are not mentioned in the bibliography by Brockelmann and Schurrer[44]. Gabriel Sionita, a Maronite priest, had already made an excellent translation of this book in 1619[45]; this leads us to think that Cremona's reference is unreliable inasmuch as it is unfounded. Since Sionita's translation, completed just seven years before, must have been available to Magri, it seems strange indeed that Magri should begin his own translation, unless he were accommodating someone else, or merely competing with Sionita. There is no doubt that Magri must have been aware of Sionita's work through his long relationship with the Maronites in Rome, who were under the patronage of Cardinal Alessandro Ursino[46]. Magri was also chosen to go to Mount Lebanon in Syria to settle certain disputes that had arisen between thc Maronites and the Vatican. Canon Magri, who was given this appointment because of his fluency in Arabic, conducted the whole affair very tactfully; the discussions were fruitful and successful, and he was much praised by both the Bishop and the Grandmaster in Malta, and the Pope in Rome.

Another prominent figure who spent most of his life travelling in the Levant was Patri Arkanġlu Zammit (1747-1812), a Franciscan, who for

[39] R. Mifsud Bonnici, *op. cit.*, p. 370.

[40] Abela-Ciantar, *op. cit.*, vol. 3, sec. 4.

[41] A. Mai, *Veterum Scriptorum Nova Collectio* (Roma: 1931), p. 476; A. Kleinhans, *op. cit.*, pp. 73-74.

[42] MS Codice Vaticano Arabo 345, p. 267.

[43] A. Cremona, *Mikiel Anton Vassalli*, p. 9.

[44] C. Brockelmann, *op. cit.*, vol. 1, p. 877; C. F. Schurrer, *op. cit.*, p. 187.

[45] *Ibid.*

[46] R. Mifsud Bonnici, *op. cit.*, p. 316.

[47] *Ibid.*

forty years occupied the post either of pastor or prior in the monasteries and parishes scattered throughout Palestine, Syria, and Egypt[48]. He translated a great number of books into Arabic, among which are the legendary life of Patri Benedetto Nazzara and, in 1690, the history of the Franciscan Saints from the Latin original[49]. Most of his manuscripts are now to be found at the Aleppo monastery in Syria, where he taught Arabic for a number of years.

An author who created a whole controversy regarding his works was Abate Giuseppe Vella (1749-1814). It is said that in 1789 Vella emigrated to Rome where, by means of an excellent reference from the Grandmaster, the Grand Prior of the Order of St. John, he managed to penetrate the higher influential circles of society[50]. He had studied Arabic in Malta before Napoleon's occupation of the island in 1798, and for some political reason, wanted to leave Malta. Bonnici says that Vella studied the language under Dun Girgor Carbone (1729-1773), but he suggests that Vella was not much interested in the subject[51].

Such a statement is misleading, because most probably he continued his studies after Carbone's death. In Rome, his goal was to be appointed lecturer at the College of the Propaganda Fide, but when he saw that it was impossible for him to realize his ambition, he went to Palermo to obtain a university lectureship there. It was here that he discovered some Arabic manuscripts dealing with the history of the Arabs in Sicily. This event generated interest all over Europe, and he immediately began his first work, a translation in six volumes, *Codice Diplomatico di Sicilia sotto il Governo degli Arabi* (Palermo, 1789-1792). This earned him the post of Professor of Arabic at the Palermo University. Later he published *Il Consiglio d'Egitto* (Palermo, 1793). These two works turned out to be a fraud[52], and for this crime Vella was condemned to fifteen years' imprisonment at the Castello di Palermo[53]. It was a harsh penalty; and although there were repeated suggestions for a thorough investigation of the fraud, no historical linguistic study of Vella's work has yet been made to examine this aspect. He died in 1814, aged 65.

[48] Abela-Ciantar, *op. cit.*, vol. 4, p. 30; Golubovich-Lemmens, *op. cit.*, p. 257; Cirelli-Mencherini, *Gli annali de Terra Sancta* (Quaracchi: 1912), p. 239.

[49] FPAM, MS A2 (i-iv).

[50] R. Mifsud Bonnici, *op. cit.*, p. 523.

[51] *Ibid.*

[52] M. Amari, *Storia dei musulmani di Sicilia*, Ed. C. A. Nallino, Vol. 1 (Catania: 1933), pp. 6-12; S. Pellegrini, "Giuseppe Vella e i suoi falsi documenti d'antichissimo rolgare", *Saggi di Filologia Italiana* (1962): 9-16; see also A. Baviera, "Il problema dell' Arabica impostura dell' Abate Vella", *Nuovi Quaderni del Meridione*, I, iv (1963): 395-428.

[53] R. Mifsud Bonnici, *op. cit.*, p. 524.

MANUSCRIPTS (ARABIC, TURKISH, PERSIAN) AND PUBLICATIONS

Arabic Manuscripts at the Archives of the Augustinian monastery, Valletta

MS 24 An Arabic grammar by Fra Agapito A Valle (d. 1687); translated from Latin into Arabic and edited by Fra Ġużeppi Grassi; dated 1877 or 1878; 391 pages.

MS (unclassified) "The Tree of Knowledge", an illustration designed by Ġużeppi Genovese, 1878.

Arabic and Turkish Manuscripts at the Cathedral Archives, Mdina

(i) Archives of the Inquisition, Malta

MS Proceeding 16, no. 5, p. 5 (1598), Ortensio. Two letters written by ʿAlī Būghriyū and Salīm al-Qandarī in Maghribī script; folded triangularly. (see illustration 2)

MS Proceeding 21, no. 26, p. 159v. (1603), Verallo. A letter in Maghribī script addressed to ʿAbd Allāh in Sūsa; folded triangularly. (see illustration 3)

MS Proceeding 23, no. 303 (s.d.), Verallo. A magical writing; folded in goatskin.

MS Proceeding 24, p. 2 (1605), Diotallevi. A prayer for the liberation of slaves in Malta; written in Turkish (document).

MS Proceeding 26 (2), no. 66 (1603), Diotallevi. "On the Practice of Magic", by Salīm b. Manṣūr.

MS Proceeding 29, no. 44 (1612), Carbonesio. A confession made by a Christian who had been forced to accept Islām.

MS Proceeding 61, no. 208, pp. 1044-1047 (1649), Pignatelli. "On the Practice of Magic and the Evil Eye", by ʿĀisha.

MS Proceeding 76, no. 76, p. 37 (s.d.), Bichi. A magical writing with verses from the Qur'ān (see 94: 1-8; 9: 128-129).

MS Correspondence 37, pp. 258-259. A letter from Bishop Agnatios of Ḥomṣ, Syria (document).

MS (unclassified). The Qur'ān with marginal notes in Arabic, Turkish, Persian, Balūchī, and Pashtū. Interment prayers according to Islamic tradition.

(ii) Cathedral Archives, Malta

MS Fondo Panzavecchia (Miscellanee supplimentari di Missali), pp. 1-2.
(i) The *Credo* in Maltese, written in Arabic script.
(ii) The *Credo* in Maltese, written in Latin and Arabic scripts.

MS Fondo Panzavecchia, p. 1. Sermons in Maltese, Latin, and Arabic (excerpts from the Gospels).

Arabic, Turkish and Persian Manuscripts at the Archives of the Order of St. John, National Library, Valletta

MS vol. 6504. Two letters written in Turkish sent by Sulṭān Muḥammad IV (1647-1687) to the functionaries of the Order (dated 1086/1675-76).

MS vol. 63. A letter in Persian from Shāh Ḥusayn I (1694-1722) to Grandmaster Fra Ramon Perellos y Roccafull (1697-1720), written in the month of Rajab, 1108/1697.

MS vol. 1202, p. 98. A letter in Turkish from ʿAbdī Ağa, Captain of the Ottoman Navy to Grandmaster Fra Don Anton Manuel de Vilhena (1722-1736), written in 1722.

MS vol. 1202, p. 95. A letter in Turkish written by Aḥmad Paşa Karamanlī 1714.

MS vol. 1206, pp. 49, 84, 233. Letters written by ʿAlī Paşa Karamanlī in February, May, and June 1766 and March 1778 to Grandmasters Ramon Perellos y Roccafull and Fra Emmanuel de Rohan Polduc (1775-1797).

MS vol. 1233. A letter in Arabic written by a slave, Muḥammad to Grandmaster Fra Don Emmanuel Pinto de Fonçeca (1741-1773), dated 1145/1732-33.

MS vol. 6392. Three letters written in Arabic by Ḥusayn Paşa and Muḥammad Beğ of Tunis to Grandmaster Fra Don Ramon Despuiz (1736-1741), dated 1737.

MS vols. 1200-1207, p. 140. Two letters written in Arabic by Ẓāhir b. ʿUmar to Grandmaster Fra Don Emmanuel Pinto de Fonçeca, dated 1756.

MS vol. 6504. Letter of greetings from Muḥammad ʿAlī Paşa (1805-1848) of Egypt to the British General of Malta, Oakes, dated Rajab 1226/August 5, 1811.

Arabic, Turkish, and Persian Manuscripts which, prior to 1609, formed part of the Inquisition Library and are now at the Vatican Library

MS Ar. 201. The first part of the Qur'ān with an interlinear Persian translation; probably fifteenth century; the first two pages were written in the sixteenth century.

MS Ar. 204. Turkish-language copy of the Qur'ān; first few pages are missing; sixteenth century.

MS Ar. 205. A copy of the Qur'ān in Maghribī script; dated 13 Dhū 'l-Qaʿda 876/April 22, 1472.

MS Ar. 224. The second part of the Qur'ān; of Turkish origin; the first section is fifteenth century, while the second is sixteenth and seventeenth century.

MS Ar. 227. The twenty-ninth and thirtieth sections of the Qur'ān, supplemented by thirty ceremonial rites; of Turkish origin; sixteenth and seventeenth century.

MS Ar. 237. Prayers and magical writings: the *Burda* of Al-Būsīrī; in Maghribī script; sixteenth and seventeenth century.

MS Ar. 238. A collection of prayers and magical incantations; in Maghribī script; undated.

MS Ar. 302. Al-Shamsiyya by Al-Kātibī; a manual of logic with a commentary by Quṭb al-Dīn al-Taḥtānī; with several glosses; in Turkish; dated 13 Shawwāl 978 and 17 Rabīʿ 979/March 10 and September 8, 1571.

MS Ar. 370. A collection of spiritual and magical writings; the night vision of the Prophet Muḥammad; written by ʿAbd al-Raḥmān b. Makhlūf al-Thʿālibī from Algeria; the *Burda* of al-Būsīrī; sixteenth century.

MS Turc. 3. A book of common prayers; mid-sixteenth century.

MS Turc. 4. Same; last pages defaced.

Ms Turc. 6. *Ibid.*

MS Turc. 26. A version of a romance, or Turkish epic about Sayyid Baṭṭāl; mid-sixteenth century.

MS Turc. 31. *Qiyāfet Nāmeh*, a short treatise on physiognomy, by Muḥammad b. Iyās; sixteenth century.

MS Turc. 352. Selections from a poem; author unknown.

Arabic and Turkish Manuscripts at the National Library, Malta

MS 16. Miscellaneous papers; *Duʿā'*, prayers alternating with verses from the Qur'ān; begins with Chapter 6, Sūrat al-Anʿām, up to verse

96; attributive invocations to Allāh; pp. 112-116; prayers in Arabic and Turkish; undated, probably fifteenth century, in Naskhī script (116 pages, 140 × 90 mm).

MS 17. The *Ecclesiastes*, translated into Turkish; two volumes; (1) thirty-six chapters, thirty-two of which have a French version; dated 23 Jumāda 1, 1190/July 10, 1776; (2) fifty-one chapters, dated 3 Ṣafar 1191/March 13, 1777 (182 and 249 pages, 210 × 140 mm).

MS 22. The Qur'ān, in Naskhī script (257 pages, 30 × 20 mm).

MS 23. *Maqāmāt*, enigmatic verses explained in rhyming prose by Abū 'l-Faḍl b. Muḥammad al-Ghasafī al-Shāfiʿī. *Al-Maqāmāt*, eulogising Mawlānā Shaykh al-Islām, Qāḍī 'l-Quḍāt Shihāb al-Dīn Aḥmad al-Anṣārī, the Vice-Sulṭān of the Ottoman Empire; dated 12 Dhū 'l-Ḥijja 997/October 22, 1589, in Naskhī script (21 pages, 200 × 150 mm).

MS 47. An incomplete Maltese dictionary written in Arabic script; date and author unknown.

MS 66. *Jiḥān Nūma* of Kātib Çelebi; in Turkish; a description of coloured maps; undated; in Ruqʿī script (357 pages, 310 × 180 mm).

MS 113. Chronological extracts of the Turkish victory of 1551, under the command of Rayyis Darghūṭ Pāşā, and the news from Tripoli and Fezzan in the sixteenth, seventeenth, and eighteenth centuries; written in Arabic by Muṣṭafā Hoca b. Kāsim, first secretary of ʿAlī Pāşā Karamanlī; with a French version, *Histoire Abrégé de Tripoly de Barbarie* by A.C. Froment, Consul of France in 1794 (49 pages, 240 × 180 mm).

MS 218. An Italian-Arabic and Italian-Arabic-Turkish dictionary in four volumes written by Dun Ġużepp Calleja (d. 1798); undated (3116 pages).

MS 346. Novels by Salvatore Muzzi (1807-1884), translated from Italian into Arabic and from Arabic into Maltese, under the pseudonym of ʿAyn Wāw; dated 1860 (126 pages, 260 × 150 mm).

MS 516. An Arabic-Italian dictionary compiled by Giuseppe Grassi; undated (2211 pages).

Arabic Manuscripts at the Franciscan Provincial Library, Valletta

MS Al. *Kitāb al-Ājurrūmiyya*, written by Dā'ūd al-Ṣinhājī, copied by the slave ʿAlī b. Yaḥyā al Zawāwī Bū Yūsuf for Patri Franġisk Flieles, O.F.M.; dated 24 Rajab 1040/February 26, 1631 (270 pages, 160 × 110 mm).

MS A2. *Tawārīkh al-Fransiskāniyya* The History of the Franciscan Saints, translated from Latin into Arabic by Patri Arkanġlu Zammit, O.F.M., in four volumes (vol. 1, 680 pages; vol. 2, 548 pages; vol. 3, 712 pages; vol. 4, 825 pages; 210 × 150 mm). A copy of this translation is found at Aleppo, in Syria; vol. 1 is dated 1690.

MS A3. A grammatical analysis; incomplete and first pages missing; probably also written by the slave ʿAlī b. Yaḥyā; dated 27 Shawwāl 1042/May 7, 1632 (162 pages, 202 × 140 mm).

MS A4. Extracts from the Gospels with explanatory notes written by Patri Giovanni Pawlu Deguara, O.F.M. (200 pages, 220 × 160 mm).

MS A5. Extracts from the Gospels and Epistles for Sundays and Feastdays; author unknown, probably eighteenth century.

MS A6. Extracts from the Gospels and Epistles for Sundays; undated, author unknown; bound in leather (140 pages, 220 × 160 mm).

MS A7. A catechism written by the slave ʿAlī b. Yaḥyā, under the direction of Patri Franġisk Flieles, O.F.M. (38 pages, 210 × 140 mm).

MS A8. Psalm 151, copied by the slave ʿAlī b. Yaḥyā; dated 1 Muḥarram 1043/July 8, 1633; bound in parchment (286 pages, 231 × 170 mm).

MS A9. A list of nouns and verbs, written by the slave ʿAlī b. Yaḥyā, under the direction of Patri Franġisk Flieles, dated 6 Ramaḍān 1039/April 19, 1629; bound in parchment (570 pages, 240 × 180 mm).

MS A10. The Gospel according to St. John, with a grammatical analysis written by ʿAlī b. Yaḥyā; undated; bound in parchment (400 pages, 270 × 210 mm).

MS All. Extracts from the Gospel according to St. John, with a grammatical analysis written by ʿAlī b. Yahyā, under the direction of Patri Franġisk Flieles; undated; bound in parchment (490 pages, 270 × 210 mm).

MS A12. A grammatical commentary of *Kitāb al-Ājurrūmiyya*, written by Muḥammad b. Dāūd al-Ṣinhājī, copied by ʿAlī b. Yaḥyā for Patri Franġisk Flieles; undated (222 pages, 278 × 210 mm).

MS A13. Psalm 151 (according to the Hebrew tradition); supplemented by grammatical notes written by ʿAlī b. Yaḥyā for Patri Franġisk Flieles; undated (160 pages, 270 × 220 mm).

MS A14. A grammatical analysis of extracts from the Gospel according to St. Matthew; undated and author unknown (295 pages, 280 × 200 mm).

MS A15. A grammatical analysis copied by ʿAlī b. Yaḥyā; dated 1041/1630 (80 pages, 276 × 210 mm).

MS A16. A commentary on the Kitāb al-ʿAwāmil, a grammatical analysis by ʿAbd al-Raḥmān al-Jurjānī; dated 27 Ramaḍān 1039/May 10, 1629 (110 pages, 278 × 210 mm).

MS A18. An Italian-Arabic dictionary (for familiar conversation) compiled by Patri Giovanni Pawlu Deguara, O.F.M., undated; bound in leather (184 pages, 240 × 160 mm).

MS A19. A list of verbs in Italian and Arabic, following the Italian alphabetical order by Patri Giovanni Pawlu Deguara, O.F.M., undated; bound in leather (261 pages, 230 × 160 mm).

MS A20. Notes on the Arabic language written by Patri Giovanni Pawlu Deguara, O.F.M., undated; bound in leather (213 pages, 220 × 160 mm).

MS A21(i). An Arabic-Italian dictionary, following the Arabic alphabetical order, compiled by Patri Giovanni Pawlu Deguara, O.F.M., dated 1848; bound in leather (675 pages, 230 × 160 mm).

MS A21(ii). An Italian-Arabic dictionary following the Italian alphabetical order, compiled by Patri Giovanni Pawlu Deguara, O.F.M., dated 1848; bound in leather (652 pages, 230 × 160 mm).

MS 345. An Arabic grammar by Patri Ludovico Muscat, O.F.M., with an interlinear Latin version; a microfilm of the Codice Vaticano Arabo (267 pages).

MS (unclassified). An Arabic grammar written by Fra Agapito A Valle (d. 1687); translated from Latin into Italian with several notes by Fra Ġużeppi Grassi; dated 1856 (391 pages).

Arabic Manuscripts at the National Museum, Valletta

MS (unclassified). The Qur'ān; incomplete; written in Maghribī script; with gold titles.

MS (unclassified). An Arabic-Italian vocabulary in two volumes by Gaetano Ciancio; undated (400 pages).

MS (unclassified). An Arabic grammar written by Fra Agapito A Valle; translated from Latin into Italian by Fra Ġużeppi Grassi; dated 1868.

Books in Arabic at the Franciscan Provincial Library, Valletta

The *Gospels*: Latin and Arabic Versions. Interlinear, a translation, probably by Antonius Sionita. Roma: Medicea, 1591.

The *Psalms*: Latin and Arabic Versions. Roma: Stephanus Paulinus ex Typographia Sawiana, 1614.

Thomae Obicini, *Grammatica Arabica.* Roma: Sacra Congregazione de Propaganda Fide, 1631 (two copies).

Fabrica ovvero dittionario della lingua volgare, arabica et italiana. Roma: Sacra Congregazione de Propaganda Fide, 1636.

Annalium Sacrorum a Creatione Mundi ad Christi D.N. Incarnationem Epitome, Latino-Arabica. Roma: Josephum Lunam Maronitam, 1655. (The name of Patri Isodor Rapa, O.F.M., is written on the cover).

Imitatio Christi. Roma: Sacra Congregazione de Propaganda Fide, 1663.

Biblia Sacra Arabica. Interlinear, vols. 1-3. Roma: Sacra Congregazione de Propaganda Fide, 1671.

Emmanuele Sanz, *Trattato nel quale con ragioni dimostratione si convincono manifestamente i Turchi, senza che in guisa veruna possano negarlo, esser falsa la legge di maometto e vera solamente quella di Cristo.* Catania: 1691.

Al-Kitāb al-Muqaddas. London: Richard Watts, 1831 (first edition 1671). (The name of Patri Giovanni Pawlu Deguara is written on the cover.)

Al-Kitāb al-Muqaddas. London: William Watts, 1838 (first edition 1671). (The name of Patri Deguara is written on the cover.)

Agapito A Valle, *Flores Grammaticales Arabici Idiomatis.* Roma: Sacra Congregazione de Propaganda Fide, 1845.

Arabic Press, Malta, 1821-1844

Thalāthu Rasā'il Mār Yuḥanna (Three Letters of St. John, extracted from the *Biblia Sacra Arabica*, Rome, 1671). Malta: 1828; 24 pages, 1; BML No. T. 2110. (2)

Amthāl (The Parables of Christ as found in the Gospels, with supplementary notes; extracted from the *Biblia Sacra Arabica*, Rome, 1671). Malta: 1828; 180 pages; BML No. 14500.D.13.

Tafsīr Muthul (The Parable of the Sower as found in the Gospel according to St. Matthew, with a brief commentary). Malta: 1829; 19 pages; BML No. 14500.aa.25.

Tawārīkh (Historial extracts from the Old Testament, with various reflections in between; extracted from the *Biblia Sacra Arabica*, Rome, 1671). Malta: 1833; 380 pages; BML No. 14500.b.11; another copy BML No. 14500.b.5.

Khabariyyāt As'ad al-Shidyāq (An account of the death of As'ad al-Shidyāq in Lebanon). Malta: 1833.

Al-Kanz al-Mukhtār (A manual of basic geography). Malta: 1833; iv, 164 pages; BML No. 14565.b.21; another copy, which is illustrated, BML No. 14565.b.14.

Amthāl Sulaymān (Selections from the Book of Proverbs, extracted from the *Biblia Sacra Arabica*, Rome, 1671, with a supplementary version in French). Malta: 1834; 48 pages; BML No. 14500.aa.35/11.

Pilgrim's Progress (Translated into Arabic, probably by Aḥmad Fāris al-Shidyāq). Malta: 1834.

Āyāt Mukhtāra (Biblical extracts for scholastic use, from the *Biblia Sacra Arabica*, Rome, 1671). Malta: 1835; 118 pages; BML No. T. 2110 (12); another copy BML No. 14505.c.2b.

Ṭarīqa Mustaḥdatha (A manual of Arabic script printed on coloured paper and set on cardboard). Malta: 1835(?); BML No. 14546.f.1.

Qiṣṣat Rubinsūn Kruzī (The Adventures of Robinson Crusoe). Malta: 1835; 252 pages.

Baḥth al-Maṭālib (Arabic grammar). Malta: 1836; 317 pages; BML No. 14593.b.2; another copy BML No. 14593.b.3.

Al-Bākūrāt al-Shahiyya (An English grammar in Arabic). Malta: 1836; 104 pages; BML No. 14586.e.7.

Risālat Mār Buṭrus (The Epistles of St. Paul, extracted from the *Biblia Sacra Arabica*, Rome, 1671). Malta: 1837(?); 24 pages; BML No. T. 2110. (5)

Fattishū 'l-Kutub al-Muqaddasa (A translation from Book No. 23 of the Religious Tract Society — First Series Tracts). Malta: 1838; 22 pages; BML No. 14500.aa.35.

Al-Lafīf fī Kull Ma'nā Ẓarīf (Elementary reading passages in Arabic). Malta: 1839; 297, 2 pages; BML No. 14586.a.15.

Book of Common Prayer (A catechism manual translated into Arabic, probably by Aḥmad Fāris al-Shidyāq or F. Schlienz). Malta: 1840.

Al-Zāri' (The Parables of Jesus Christ). Malta: 1840; 236 pages; BML No. 14505.c.15.

Al-Muḥāwarāt al-Unsiyya (Grammar exercises in English and Arabic, with everyday conversations intended for English students). Malta: 1840; 188 pages; BML No. 14586.d.7; another copy BML No. 14586.e.1.

Sharḥ Ṭabāi' al-Ḥayāwān (A book on natural history translated from English into Arabic). Malta: 1841; first volume, 349 pages; BML No. 14533.a.11.

Al-Ajwibat al-Jāliyya (An elementary textbook for the study of Arabic extracted from *Baḥth al-Maṭālib*). Malta: 1841; 123 pages; BML No. 14593.c.33.

Faṣl al-Khiṭāb (A treatise on the homilies of Jibrīl Farḥat, with supplementary comments and three sermons by Rev. C. Simeon). Malta: 1842; 373 pages; BML No. 14505.c.2.

Al-Taqnīʿ fī 'l-Badīʿ (An epitome of *Khizānat al-Adab*; a treatise on Ibn Ḥijja (d. 837/1434) written by Fāris b. Manṣūr al-Shidyāq). Malta: 1843; 177 pages, 22.3 × 15.7 cm; Chester Beatty Library MS 4099.

Atlas (A mapbook intended for scholastic use, by F. Brockdorff). Malta: 1835.

Lecturers of Arabic in Malta, 1632-1915

1632-1633	Patri Franġisku Flieles, O.F.M.
1637-1652	Patri Duminku Pace, O.F.M.
1637-1643	Dun Franġisk Azzopardi
(?)-1680	Patri Anġlu Xerri, O.F.M.
1643-1683	Dun Salvu Fenech
1684-1729	Dun Fabrizju Bonnici
1729-1773	Dun Girgor Carbone
1773-1798	Dun Ġużepp Calleja
1788-1798(?)	Mikiel Anton Vassalli
1803-(?)	Antonio Faḍl Allāh
1805-1807	Patri Anastasju, O.F.M.
1807-1838	Fra Ġużeppi Grassi, O.S.J.
1838-1848	Aḥmad Fāris al-Shidyāq
1853-1853	Robertu Casolani
1853-1881	Geitanu Ciancio
1881-1889	Robertu Casolani
1889-1895	Antonju Sarreo
1895-1914/15	Dun Yūsuf Sebhlani

APPENDIX

Document 1

Archives of the Inquisition, Malta. Correspondence of the Sacra Congregazione de Propaganda Fide. Vol. 1.
A.I.M. 1628-1726. Cor. Sec. 36, p. 1r.

Illustrissimo e Molto Rev. do Signore

Essendo stato deputato per lator della lingua Araba in questa isola fra Francesco da Malta Minore Osservante, questa Sacra Congregazione, che graditamente (?) dichiara l'eretione e continuazione dello Studio della suddetta lingua, ha voluto che io a V.S. raccomandi come con ogni efficacia faccio, la persona del suddetto Padre accio l'agiusti, e col Gran Maestro e con Mons. Vescovo per l'efformazione del desiderio della medesima Sac. Congregazione incaricando V.S. della sorveliantia doveroso del medesimo studio, sino che questa lodevole opera si principii e proseguisca a gloria di Dio, et in salute di molte animi che per difetto di operarii che sappino la suddetta lingua stanno in pericolo della loro salvazione che quanto opererà nel sud. parte sarà accreditato (?) alla medesima Sac. Congregazione per nome della quale a V.S. mi offro e raccomando.

da Roma, 13 feb. 1628.

aff.mo
Card. Bandini.

A Mons. Inquisitore di Malta

Francesco Ingoli, sec.

Document 2

Archives of the Propaganda Fide, Rome
Acta 1629, p. 240.

Referente eodem Ill.mo D. Card. S. Sixti difficultates quas haec erectio studii linguae Arabicae in Melita Insula apud Minores de Observantia S. Congr. iussit scribi Inquisitori et Episcopo eiusdem Insula, ut curent difficultates praesentes removeri, ac erigi presentem studium, et simul praecepit agi cum Commissario Generali pro eisdem difficultatibus tollendis.

A tergo: Studium Linguae Arabicae in Melita Insula impeditur.

Document 3

Archives of the Propaganda Fide, Rome
Letters, Vol. 8, p. 49 r-v.

Al vescovo et inquisitore di Malta.

Quanto più pare che si frapponghino difficoltà nell'erettione dello studio Arabico in cotesta Città, tanto più sarà opportuno il favore et aguito che V.S. ha promesso al P. Francesco di Malta per il medesimo effetto, e sicome questa S. Congregazione sperimenta che tutte le opere buone al principio hanno sempre qualche intoppo, cosi non ha mancato di fare il possibile col Padre Commissario Generale dei Minori Osservanti, acciò faccia la parte sua per promuovere quest'opera, sicome ha promesso di fare nel capitolo che si celebrerà fatto Pasqua. Intanto V.S. animerà il sudetto Padre a non desistere dall'incominciata impresa: perchè da tutte le parti sarà aguitato a proseguirla, et a mantenerla e con questo fine ringrazindola dalle cortesi offerte, che elle gli/ha fatto.

D.V.S. ecc Roma, 17 Marzo, 1629.

Document 4

Archives of the Propaganda Fide, Rome
Letters, Vol. 12, p. 31 r-v.

Ha sentito particolare piacere questa Sacra Congregazione che V. R. habbia/ incominciato a leggere la lingua arabica e sicome desidera di vederne lo sperato frutto, che si sodisfacci al istanza sia con decretarli quattro salteri Arabici, e due Vangeli simili con 6 Grammatiche del Padre Tommaso da Novara, le quali in una balletta s'invieranno al Sig. Cassano Giustino in Messina acciò le mandi a cotesto Monsignore Inquisitore per renderle poi in mano di V.R., a cui, ecc. Roma, 20 Marzo, 1632.

Document 5

Archives of the Inquisition, Correspondence of the Sac. Cong. de Propaganda Fide. Vol. 1.
A.I.M. 1628-1726. Corr. Sec. 36, p. 125 r.

Ill.mo e Rev.mo mio Sig.re Oss.mo

Tengo avviso da più parti di buoni portamenti che fa Fra Francesco da Malta Vice-commissario di Terra Santa costi, perciò sono in obligo di raccomandarle alla protettione di VS Ill.ma, come faccio permezzo della presente, supplicandolo a restar servita, d'esserli liberali nell'onoranze del suo patrocinio maggiormente si per emulatione dei frati, che circa quest'ufficio di commisariato di Terra Santa non mancano (corr. 'fosse travagliato') secondo io che sono pro secretario della Sac. Cong. de Sacri Luoghi, spisso querel — de' distrubi ed impedimenti che li commissari e loro compagni ricevono dalli superiori locali, VS ill.ma che è in fatto saprà meglio di me li buone qualità del detto Fra Francesco e perciò mi assicura che farà nel favorirlo più di quello io possa desiderare. E per fine a V.S. Ill.ma bacio umilmente le mani.

Roma il 18 gennaro 1645.

di V.S. Ill.ma e Rev.ma

Umillissimo e devotissimo
Francesco Ingoli, sec.

a Mons. Inquisitore di Malta.

Document 6

Archives of the Inquisition, Correspondence of the Sac. Cong. de Propaganda Fide. Vol. 2.
A.I.M. 1628-1726. Cor. Sec. 37, p. 318.

(Lo studio della lingua araba)

... non solo è profittevole ma anzi è necessario specialmente per questa Sacra Inquisizione per non essere costretta nei casi rilevanti, che sogliono accadere a servigli di Schiavi infedeli e persone vili per interpreti ... per l'istruzione che ne prendono i continui religiosi che passano in Levante per le Missioni, e per trattenersi né Luoghi di Terra Santa ... e com'è seguito specialmente in più scolari del presente lettore Canonico (Fabrizio) Bonnici, tra quali il P. Filippo Spagnuolo Minore Osservante, che mediante simile idioma e carattere si è reso assai singolare nelle parti d'Oriente ...

30 Settembre, 1724.

BIBLIOGRAPHY

ABELA, Giovanni Francesco. *Malta illustrata; ovvero descrizione di Malta isola del mare siciliano e adriatico, con le sue articlità*. Revised by G.A. Ciantar. Vols. 1-2. Malta: F.G. Mallia, 1772-80.

AGIUS, Dionisius. "Maltese: A Semitic and Romance Language". *Al-'Arabiyya* 13 (1980): 14-27.

AMARI, Michele. *Storia dei musulmani di Sicilia*. Edited C.A. Nallino. Vols. 1-3. Catania: R. Prampolini, 1933-39.

AQUILINA, Joseph. *Papers in Maltese Linguistics*. Malta: University Press, 1970 [a reprint of 1961 edition].

ARBERRY, Arthur John. "Fresh light on Ahmad Faris al-Shidyaq", *Islamic Culture* 26, i (1952): 155-168.

AZZOPARDI, Vincenzo. *Raccolta di varie cose article e moderne, utile ed interessanti riguardanti Malta e Gozo*. Malta: n.p., 1843.

BAUMGARTEN, Paul Maria. *Neue Kunde von alten Bibeln*. Roma: F. Cuggiani, 1922.

BAVIERA, A. "Il problema dell' Arabica impostura dell' Abate Vella". *Nuovi Quaderni del Meridione* 1, iv (1963): 395-428.

Biblioteca bio-bibliografica della Terra Santa e dell' Oriente francescano. Ed. G. Golubovich. Vol. 1. Quaracchi: Collegio di S. Bonaventura, 1921.

BONNICI, Arthur. *History of the Church in Malta*. Vols. 1-3. Malta: Catholic Institute, 1967-1975.

BORG, Vincent. *The Seminary of Malta and the Ecclesiastical Benefices of the Maltese Islands*. Malta: Sr. Joseph's Home, 1965.

BROCKELMANN, Carl. *Geschichte der Arabischen Litteratur*. Vols. 1-2. Leiden: E.J. Brill, 1943-49; [first edition, 1898-1902].

——. *Geschichte der Arabischen Litteratur. Supplement*. Vols. 1-3. Leiden: E.J. Brill, 1937-42.

CACHIA, Pierre. "An Arab's view of 19th century Malta. From Shidyaq's 'Al-Wāṣitah li-Ma'rifat Aḥwāl Māliṭah'". *Maltese Folklore Review* 1, i (1962): 62-69.

Catalogo dei codici e dei manoscritti inediti che si conservano nella Publica Biblioteca di Malta. Compiled by C. Vassallo. Malta, 1856.

Catalogue of Arabic Books in the British Museum. Compiled by A.G. Ellis. Vol. 1. London, 1967.

Catalogue of Books in the Public Library of Malta. Vols. 1-2. Malta, 1912.

CAMILLERI, Joseph J. "The abolition of the class of Arabic at the Lyceum". *Melita Historica* 7, ii (1977): 171-174.

CIRELLI, Antonio. *Gli annali de Terra Santa*. Edited S. Mencherini. Quaracchi: Collegio di S. Bonaventura, 1918.

CREMONA, Antonio. "L'Antica fondazione della scuola di lingua araba in Malta". *Melita Historica* i, ii-iv (1953): 3-21.

——. *Mikiel Anton Vassalli u Żminijietu*. Malta: Klabb Kotba Maltin, 1975.

FENECH, Edward. "Malta's contribution towards Arabic studies". *Actes du*

Premier Congrès d'Études des Cultures Méditerranéennes d'Influence Arabo-Berbère. (Algiers: S.N.E.D., 1973): 256-260.

FERRES, Achille. *Descrizione storica delle chiese di Malta e Gozo*. Malta: n.p., 1866.

FLEISCHER, Heinrich Lebrecht. "Eine newarabische Kaside". *Zeitschrift der Deutschen Morgenländischen Gesellschaft* 5 (1851): 249-257.

FSADNI, Mikiel. *Il Miġja u l-Ħidma ta' l-Ewwel Dumnikani f'Malta (1450-1512)*. Malta: Lux Press, 1965.

FÜCK, Johann. "Geschichte der semitischen sprachwissenschaft". *Semitistik — Handbuch der Orientalistik* Vol. 3. (Leiden, 1964): 31-39.

GALBIATI, Giovanni. "La prima stampa in arabo" in *Miscellanea Giovanni Mercati* Vol. 6. (Vatican, 1946): 409-413.

GOLUBOVICH, G. *Biblioteca bio-bibliografica della Terra Santa e dell' Oriente Francescano*. Vol. 1. Quaracchi: Collegio di S. Bonaventura, 1921.

A Handlist of the Arabic Manuscripts in the Chester Beatty Library. Compiled by A.J. Arberry. Dublin, 1962.

HILLS, Margaret T. "Languages of the Near East 1831-1860". *Missionary Research Library American Bible Society*. (Manuscript). New York, N.Y., 1964.

Historical Catalogue of the Printed Editions of Holy Scripture in the Library of the British and Foreign Bible Society. Compiled by T.H. Darlow and H.F. Moule. London: The Bible House, 1903-11.

HITTI, Philip K. *The First Book Printed in Arabic*. Princeton: University Press, 1942.

HOLZAPFEL, Heribert. *Manuale historiae Ordinis Fratrum Minorum*. Trans. from Latin by G. Haselbeck. Freiburg, Breisgan: Herder, 1909.

KEENAN, Patrick Joseph. *Malta. Report upon the Educational System of Malta*. London: Eyre-Spottiswoode, 1880.

KLEINHAUS, Ardninus. *Historia studii linguae Arabicae et Collegii missionum Ordinis fratrum minorum in conventu ad S. Petrum in Monte Aureo Romae*. Vol. 1. Quracchi: Collegio di S. Bonaventura, 1930.

LAFERLA, Albert V. *British Malta*. Vols. 1-2. Malta, 1947.

LANTSCHOOT, A. van. "Lettre inéditée de Thomas Obicini à Pietro della Valle". *Revista degli Studi Orientali* 28 (1953): 118-129.

LEE, Hilda J. *Malta 1813-1914*. Malta: Progress Press, 1972.

LEVI DELLA VIDA, Giorgio. *Ricerche sulla formazione del più antico dei manoscritti orientali della biblioteca vaticana*. Vatican: Biblioteca Apostolica Vaticana, 1939.

List of Manuscripts and Other Records Preserved amongst the Various Collections of the 'Archivio Apostolico Vaticano', Bearing on the History of Malta, with Special Reference to the Order of St. John of Jerusalem and to the Inquisition in Malta. Compiled by Hannibal Scicluna. Malta, 1932.

MALLIA, Pawlu. *Il-Giżwiti*. Malta: Injazjana, 1970.

MARSHALL, David. *History of the Maltese Language in Local Education*. Malta: University Press, 1971.

MICHEL, Ersilio. "I manoscritti della Biblioteca Vaticana relativa alla storia di Malta". *Archivio Storico di Malta* 1, ii (1930): 152-169.

——. "I manoscritti della Biblioteca Nazionale di Parigi relativi alla storia di Malta". *Archivio Storico di Malta* 2, i (1930): 76-88.

——. "I manoscritti delle Biblioteche di Roma relativi alla storia di Malta". *Archivio Storico di Malta* 3, i-iv (1932): 115-142.

——. "I manoscritti del 'British Museum' relativi alla storia di Malta". *Archivio Storico di Malta* 4, ii-iv (1934): 137-144.

MIFSUD, Alfredo. "Appunti sugli archivi di Malta". *Archivum Melitense* 2, xiii-xvi (1912-13): 9-67.

MIFSUD, Ignazio Saverio. *Biblioteca Maltese*. Malta: Niccolò Capaci, 1764.

MIFSUD BONNICI, Robert. *Dizzjunarju bijo-Bibljografiku Nazzjonali*. Malta: Dipartiment ta' l-Informazzjoni, 1960.

MIZZI, Angelo. *L'Apostolato maltese nei secoli passati con speciale riguardo all' azione missionaria svolta nel bacino mediterraneo*. Vol. 1. Malta, 1937.

MIZZI, Giuseppe. "Spigolando fra documenti inediti (sec. xvii-xix)". *Melita Historica* 5, i (1968): 39-56.

NASRALLAH, Joseph. *L'Imprimerie au Liban. Gravure sur bois de Zāker*. Beirut: n.p., 1948 [?]

PELLEGRINI, Silvio. "Giuseppe Vella e i suoi falsi documenti d'antichissimo volgare". *Saggi di Filologia Italiana* (1926): 9-16.

Philologia Orientalis 1. Leiden: E.J. Brill, 1976.

POZZO, Bartolomeo dal. *Historia della Sacra Religione Militare di S. Giovanni Gerosolimitano detta di Malta*. Vols. 1-2. Verona: G. Berno, 1703-1715.

ROSSI, Ettore. "Manoscritte e documenti orientali nelle biblioteche e negli archivi di Malta". *Archivio Storico di Malta* 2, i (1930): 1-10.

——. *Storica della marina dell' Ordine di San Giovanni di Gerusalemme, di Rodi e di Malta*. Roma: Società Editrice d'Arte Illustrata, 1926..

SALIBA, Issa A. "The Bible in Arabic: The 19th Century Protestant translation". *The Muslim World* 64, iv (1975): 254-263.

SCERRI, Giorgio. *Malta e i luoghi santi della Palestina*. Malta: Lux Press, 1933.

SCHLIENZ, Christoph Friedrich. *Views on the Improvement of the Maltese Language and its Use for the Purpose of Education and Literature*. Malta: n.p., 1838.

SCHURRER, Christanus de. *Biblioteca Arabica*. Amsterdam: Oriental Press, 1968.

Scriptorum veterum nova collectio e vaticanis codicibus. Compiled by A. Mai. Vols. 1-10. Rome: Typis Vaticanis, 1825-1831.

SOMIGLI, Teodosio. *Etiopia francescana nei documenti dei secoli XVII e XVIII*. Vols. 1-2. Quaracchi: Collegio di San Bonaventura, 1928-1948.

STOCK, Eugene. *The History of the Church Missionary Society*, Vols. 1-4. London, 1899.

VELLA, Andrew P. *Storja ta' Malta*. Vols. 1-2. Malta: Klabb Kotba Maltin, 1974-1979.

WETTINGER, Godfrey. "The distribution of surnames in Malta in 1419 and the 1480's". *Journal of Maltese Studies* 5 (1968): 25-48.

ZAMMIT, Temi. *Malta*. Malta: A.C. Aquilina, 1971; [first published in 1948].

ZARB, Seraphim. "The archives of Malta". *Scientia* 22, iii (1956): 97-110.

ZAYDĀN, Jurjī. *Tā'rīkh Ādāb al-Lughat al-'Arabiyya*. Vols. 1-4. Cairo: Dār al-Hilāl, 1957.

ZENKER, Julius Theodor. *Bibliotheca orientalis. Manuel de bibliographie orientale*. Vols. 1-2. Leipzig: G. Engelmann, 1844-61.

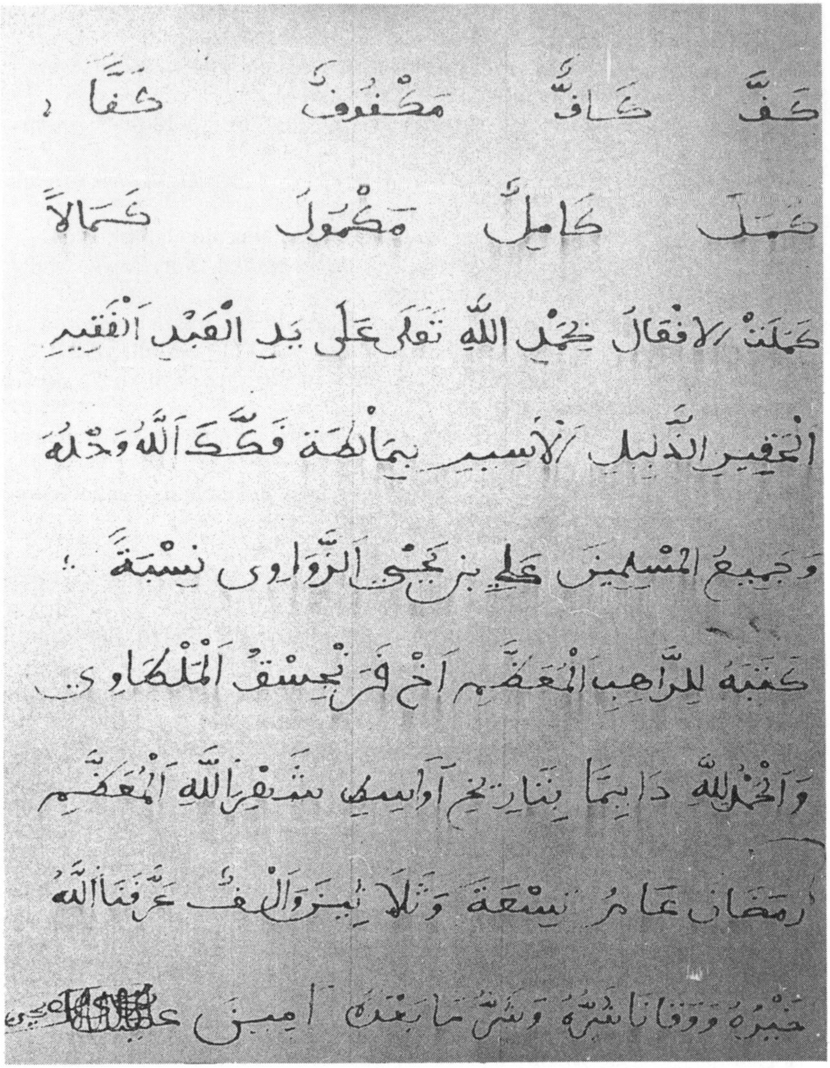
كف كاف مكفوف كفا
كمل كامل مكمول كمالا
كملت الافعال بحمد الله تعالى على يد العبد الفقير
الحقير الذليل الاسير بمالطة فكه الله وحده
وجميع المسلمين علي بن يحيى الزواوي نسبة
كتبه للراهب المعظم اخ فرنجسق الملكاوي
والحمد لله دايما بتاريخ اواسط شهر الله المعظم
رمضان عام تسعة وثلاثين والف عرفنا الله
خيره ووقانا شره وشر ما بعده امين

MS A9 "List of Nouns and Verbs" written and signed by the slave ʿAlī b. Yaḥyà 'l-Zawāwī in 1039/1629. Franciscan Library, Valletta.

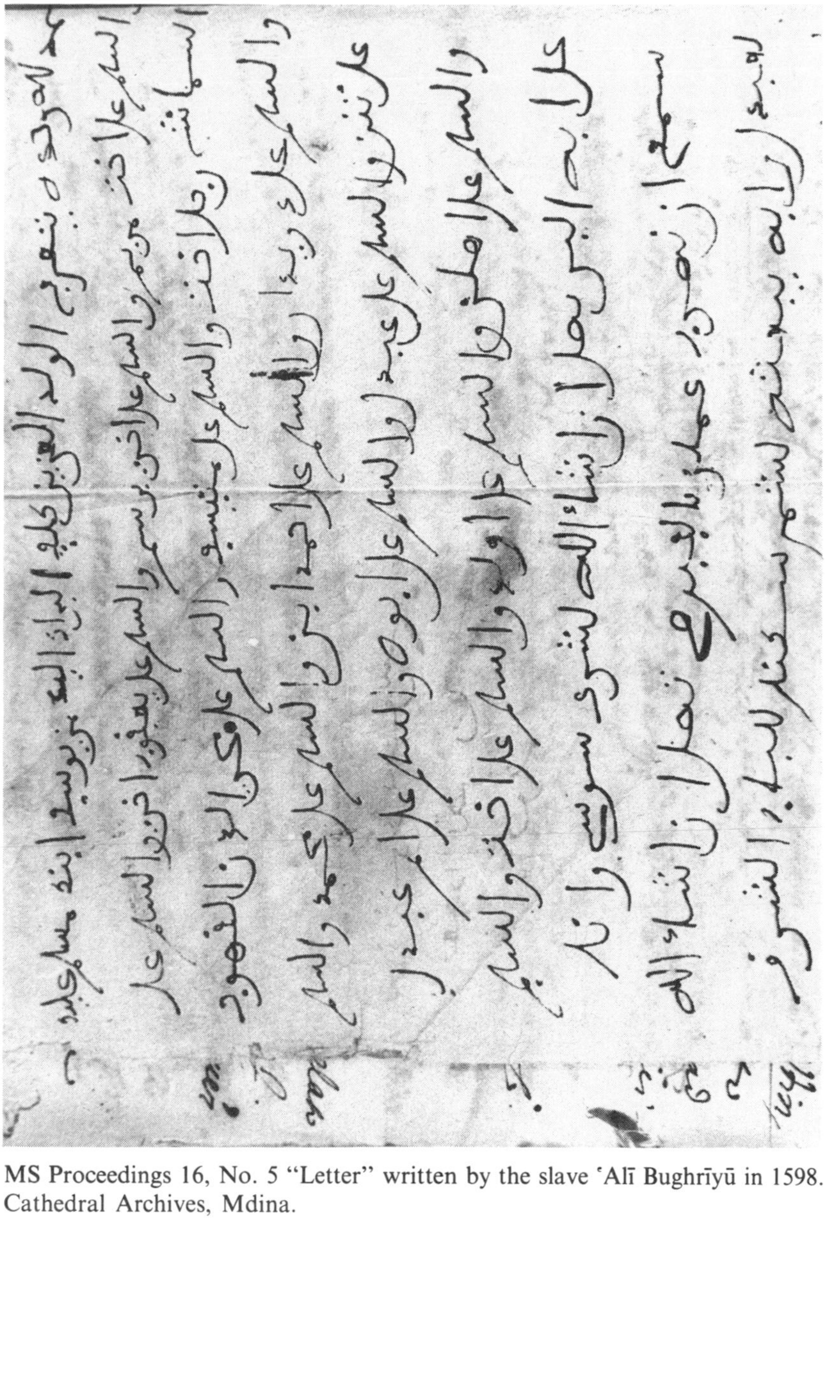

MS Proceedings 16, No. 5 "Letter" written by the slave ʿAlī Bughrīyū in 1598. Cathedral Archives, Mdina.

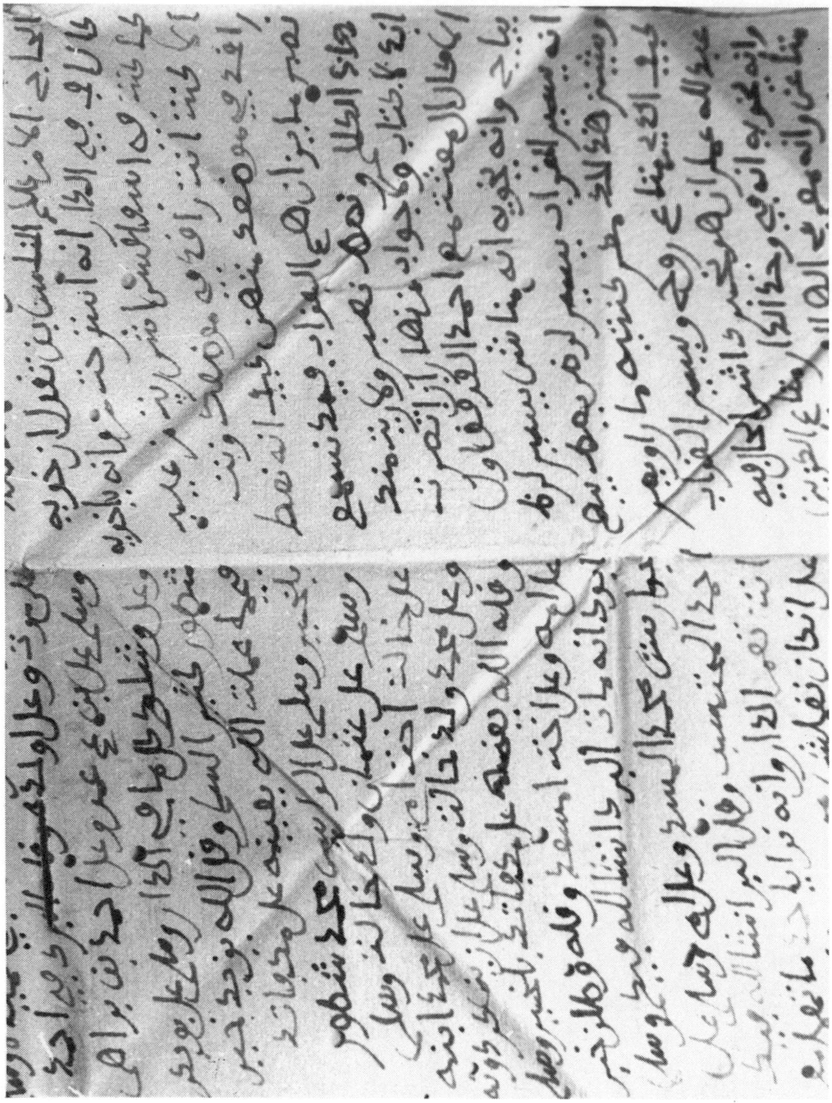

MS Proceedings 21, No. 26 "Letter" written by the slave ʿAbd Allāh in 1603. Cathedral Archives, Mdina.

INDEX

(Abel) Abela, Bishop Leonardu, 22-23
Abela, Ġan Franġisk, 23
Age of Enlightenment, xi
Agriculture, book on, 2
Ājurrūmiyya, 25-26
Aleppo, 23, 30
Alexandria, 27
Anastasio, Patri, 14
Annual prize, 5, 9
Apostolic delegate, 24
Arab(s), xi; Countries, 20, 25, 27; Muslims, 6; in Sicily, 30
Arabic, chair of, 10, 16; Classical, 14, 17; dictionary, 27; grammar, 24; Italian dictionary, 27; language and culture, 19, 22-23, 27; linguistic works, 24; Press, 18, 27-28; professor of, 12, 13, 19, 30; reader, 28; school of, 11; study of, xii, 1, 3, 6, 16, 19, 20-21; teaching of, 2, 5-7, 11-12, 14-21, 25, 27, 30; works, 22
Arabic Studies, 3; establishment of, 2, 28
Arabists, 18, 28
Arabophiles, 19, 20
Armenian-Turkish, press, 27
Arts, Faculty of, 16
Assemanno, Simone, 12
Austin, John, 15, 16
Authorities, Ecclesiastical, 4, 6-8, 16-17; lay, 16
Azzopardi, Dun Franġisk, 3-6.
Baḥth al-Maṭālib, 28
Al-Bākūrāt al-Shahiyya, 28

Ball, Captain Alexander, 13; Commissioner, 14; Rear-Admiral, Sir, 13
Beğ of Tunis, 28
Beirut, 27
Bethlehem, 27
Bible, translation of the, 28
Birgu, 3-5, 8
Bishop of Sidon, 22
Bonnici, Archdeacon Dun Mikiel, 6
Bonnici, Dun Fabrizju, 6-8
Borg, Vincenzo, 8
Borghese, Scipione, 24
Bormla, 3
Britain, 20
British, 13; administration, 14; commissioners, 16; government, 16, 18-19; officials, 16; rule, 14
Brockelmann, Carl, 29

Cagliares, Bishop, 2, 3
Cairo, 27
Calleja, Dun Ġużepp, 10-13
Camarasa, Bishop Giovanni Balagner, 4, 6
Camilleri, Dun Alwiġ, 17
Cannaves, Bishop Ġakmu, 7
Canons, 7
Carbone, Dun Girgor, 8-10, 30
Carmelite Monastery, 3
Carmelites, Discalced, 3
Carpegna, Inquisitor, 12
Casolani, Robertu, 19
Castelli, Cardinal, 9-10
Castello di Palermo, 30
Cathedral, archives at Mdina, 8; Chapter, 6
Çelebi, Süleymân, 24
Chaldean, 23, 25
Chigi, Inquisitor, 3-4
Christian Missionary Society (CMS), 27
Christianity, xi, 1, 22
Christians, 22-23
Church, Catholic, 22; Maronite, 27; Oriental, 23; Protestant, 27; unity of the, 23
Ciancio, Gejtanu, 19
Codice Diplomatico di Sicilia, 30
College of the Propaganda Fide, 3
Commissioner for the Holy Places, 4
Congregazione, see Sacra Congregazione de Propaganda Fide
Consalvi, Cardinal, 13
Il Consiglio d'Egitto, 30
Converts, xi; Muslim, xi
Cornewall Lewis, George, 15-16
Cremona, Ninu, 7, 9-10, 12, 18, 29

Da Virgoletta, Patri Antonio, 4
De Bussan, Bishop Pawlu, 8
De Hompesch, Grandmaster Ferdinand, 11
De Lascaris Castellar, Grandmaster, 4
De Rohan Polduc, Grandmaster Manuel, 11
De Schurrer, Christanus, 29; master, 4

Deguara, Patri Pawlu, 26-27
Della Corbara, Monsignor Leonetto, 24
Doctrine, religious, 17; Protestant, 27

Education, 12, 15; elementary, 15; reform, 16; system, 17, 21
Egypt, 3, 27, 30
English, grammar, 28; language, 28
Erpenius, Thomas, 24-26

Faḍl Allāh, Antonio, 13
Farḥat, Jirmānūs, 28
Fās, 25
Fenech, Dun Salvu, 5-6
Flieles, Patri Franġisk, 1-3, 25-26
Foreign Office, 14
Franciscan(s), xii, 1, 3-5, 8, 14, 25-26, 28-29, monastery, 2-3, 8; Order, 6; Province, 14; Provincial Library, 2, 5, 25-27; saints, 30
French, Commissioner of the government, 12; language, 12; occupation, 11-14
Frère, Hookham, 14-16

Galleys, 1; Ottoman, 24
General Visitor, 24
Government, colonial, 18, 20; treasurer, 14
Gozitan, farmers, 13, 21
Grassi, Gużeppi Fra, 13-16, 18, 26-27
Greek, language, 14; press, 27
Gregory XIII, Pope, 28
Għawdex, 5-6
Ħal Għargħur, 17
Hankey, Frederick, 14
Hebrew, language, 16, 19, 25; press, 27
Herrera, Inquisitor, 3
Holland, 28
Humanities, 12

Ibn Ājurrūm, Abū ʿAlī Muḥammad al-Ṣinhājī, 25
Al-Idrīsī, 29
Ingoli, Monsignor, 4
Innocent XI, Pope, 6
Inquisition, 8, 10-11, 24
Inquisitor, 9-11; Spanish, 29
Interpreter(s), 1-3, 8, 22
Isla, 5, 7
Islam, xi
Istanbul, 19, 28
Italian(s), 19; alphabet, 19; Arabic dictionary, 27; language, 16, 29; orthography, 20; phonetics, 20; press, 27; translation, 26
Italophiles, 16, 18, 19

Jacobites, 23
Jarrett, Thomas, 18, 28
Jerusalem, 27
Jesuit College, 1-2; Jesuits, 1

Keenan, P.J., 16-17; Keenan Report, 17, 19
Kitāb al-Muḥāwara, 28
Kitāb Nuzhat al-Mushtāq, 29
Kitāb Rujār, 29
Knights of the Order of Saint John, see Order of Saint John
Al-Lafīf li-Kull Maʿnā Ẓarīf, 28

Lante, Inquisitor, 10
Latakiyya, 27
Latin, culture, 23; language, 14, 25-26, 29-30
Lebanon, 18, 20, 27; Mount (see Syria)
Leiden, 24; University of, 24
Lingua franca, xi
London, 18
Lyceum, 15, 18-21, 27

Magri, Dun Domenico, 29
Mallia, Pawlu, 1
Malta, Church of, 15, 17; government of, 16; University of, 11-13, 15; University of — authorities, 16
Maltese, 14-15, 19; dialect, 15, 20; farmers, 13, 21; missionary fathers, 13; reader, 17; Semitic, 20; scholars, 20; study of, 14; teacher(s), 16-17
Mancini, Bishop Gaspare Gori, 7
Manuscripts, 30; Arabic, 22-23, 25, 28, 30; Armenian, 23; Oriental, 22; Persian, 23; Syriac, 23
Maronite(s), 20, 27, 29; rite, 20
Mattei, Bishop Ferdinandu, 14, 17
Mdina, 5, 8, 9-11, 22; Seminary, 12
Merchants, xi
Mewlid el-Nebi, 24
Mifsud Bonnici, Robertu, 20, 30
Mission, American, 27; Anglo-American, 28
Missionaries, 3
Missionary, 26; Protestant, 17; Purpose, 15
Mizzi, Ġużeppi, 2
Molina, Bishop Mikiel Ġlormu, 6
Montario, xii
Mosta, 5, 26
Muḥammad, 24
Muscat, Patri Ludwig, 28-29

Muslim(s), 1; Arabs, 6, 8; Countries, 3

Napoleon, 11-12, 30
Nationalization, 17
Nazzara, Patri Benedetto, 30
Novara, xii

Obicini, xii, 25-26, 28
Order of Saint John, 2; Grand Prior, 30; Grandmaster, 30; Knights of the, 11, 13, 23-24
Oriental Languages, 3, 11, 16, 25; Professor of, 12, 19; study of, 16
Ottoman(s), 22; Empire, xi

Pace, Patri Duminku, 3-6
Padova, 26
Palermo, 30; University, 30
Palestine, 30
Palmieri, Bishop David Cocco, 7
Papal States, Secretary for, 13
Paul V, Pope, 24
Persia, 3
Philip IV, King, 28
Pinto de Fonseca, Grandmaster Emmanuel, 11
Pius VI, Pope, 11
Prefecture, 10
Press, Arabic (see Arabic press); Medicean, 25; Media, 28
Prior of the Order, 4
Propaganda Fide, see Sacra Congregazione de Propaganda Fide; Prefect of the, 9-10; Secretary of the, 9
Propagation of the Christian Faith, 6
Publications, 18

Qaṣīda, 28
Qur'ān, 24

Rabat (Malta), 5
Raimondi, Giovanni Battista, 28
Rectorate, University, 15
Reform, academic and financial, 16
Reformation, xi
Rents for the lands and dwellings, 5, 21
Robinson, Thomas, 18, 28
Roger II of Sicily, King, 29
Rome, xi-xii, 2-3, 6-8, 10, 12-15, 20, 22-23, 25, 28-30
Ruffo, Inquisitor, 7

Sacra Congregazione de Propaganda Fide, xii, 1-11, 13-15, 20-21, 25, 28
Sacred College of Cardinals, 7
Sacripante, Cardinal, 7
San Giorgio, Cardinal, 24
San Giovanni Laterano, Basilica di, 23
San Pietro de Montario, College, 25
Sant, Dun Bert, 17
Santa Cecilia, 5
Sarbelloni, Inquisitor, 9
Sarreo, Antonio, 19
Schlienz, Reverend, 17
School(s), Central, 12; Elementary (or Primary), 14-19, 21; Valletta Government, 18
Scriptures, Holy, 17-18
Scudi, Roman, 5, 9-10, 13
Sebhlani, Reverend Yūsuf, 20
Seminarians, 7-9
Seminary, 6-8
Semitic languages, 12
Al-Shidyāq, Aḥmad Fāris, 18-19, 27-28
Sicily, 29
Sionita, Gabriel, 29
Slave(s), Muslim, 1, 23, 25-26
Society for Promoting Christian Knowledge (SPCK), 18
Society of Jesus, 1
Spain, 28-29
Spanish, Inquisitor, 29; language, 29
Sperelli, Inquisitor, 9
State, Secretary of, 14
Süleymân II Kânûnî, xi
Supreme Tribunal, 29
Syria, 3, 23, 29-30
Syriac, language, 25

Ta' l-Iskof benefice, 4, 6-7, 9, 11-13, 20
Targaman, see Interpreter
Tarxien, 11
Technical training, 12
Texts, biblical, 26; magic, 24; religious, 24; romance, 24
Treasurer, 14
Tripoli (Libya), 27
Tunisia, 13
Turkey, xi
Turkish, 1, 24
Turks, xi
Tychsen, O.G., 12

University, 19; administration, 20; Council, 18; Rector, 18
Urban VIII, Pope, xii
Urban College, 9, 13, 21; of the Propaganda Fide, 28, 30

Ursino, Cardinal Alessandro, 29

Valle, Fra Agapito A., 26
Valletta, 1, 3-6, 8, 10-11, 18, 25, 27
Van Lantschoot, A., 25
Vassallo, Cesare, 11
Vassalli, Mikiel Anton, 12
Vatican, 22-24, 29; library, 24, 29
Vella, Abate Giuseppe, 30

Wignacourt, Grandmaster, 2
World War I, 20-21

Xerri, Patri Anġlu, 5-6

Yeni çeri (Janissaries), xi

Zammit, Patri Arkanġlu, 29
Zammit, Temi, 20
Al-Zawāwī, ʿAlī b. Yaḥyā, 25-26
Żejtun, 16-17